ENGLISH WOOD-ENGRAVING 1900–1950

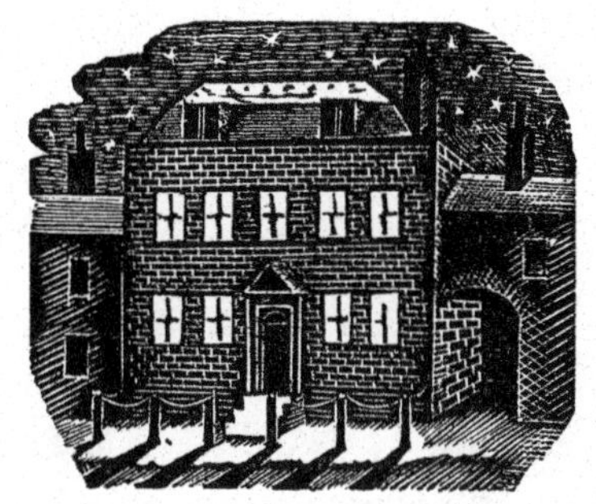

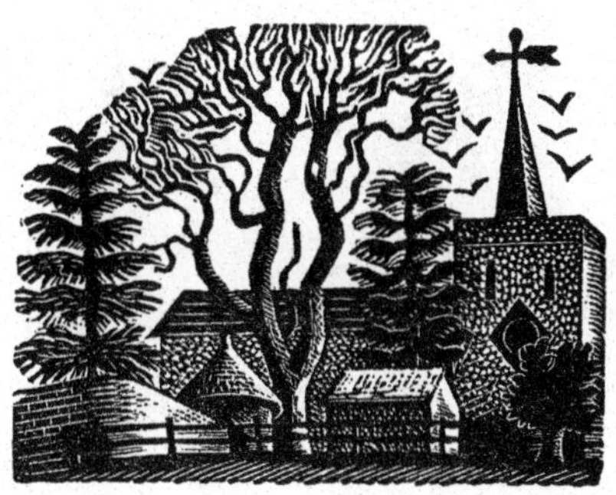

ERIC RAVILIOUS. Decorations for Kynoch Press, 1933

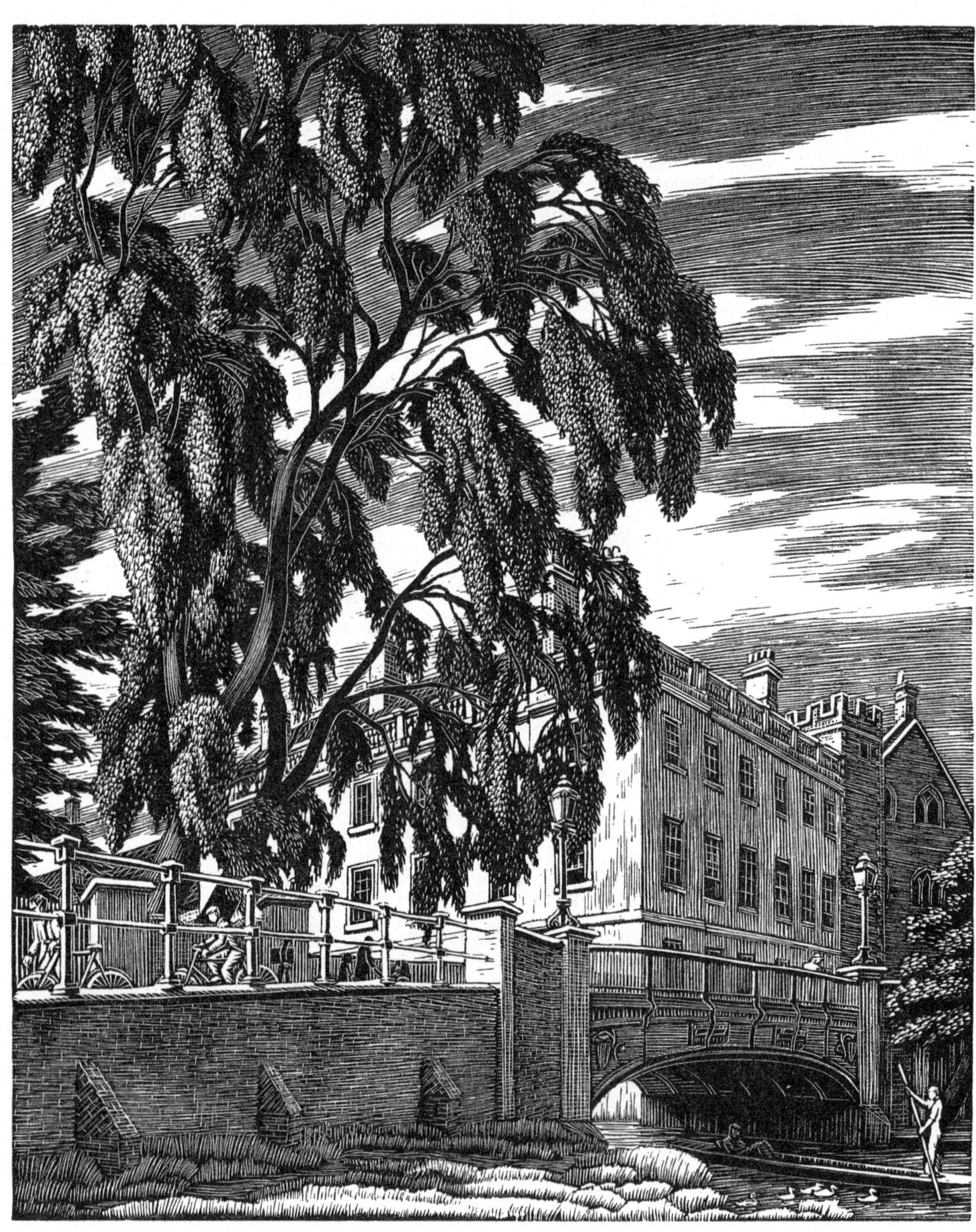

GWENDOLEN RAVERAT. Silver Street, Cambridge, 1938

ENGLISH WOOD-ENGRAVING 1900–1950

THOMAS BALSTON

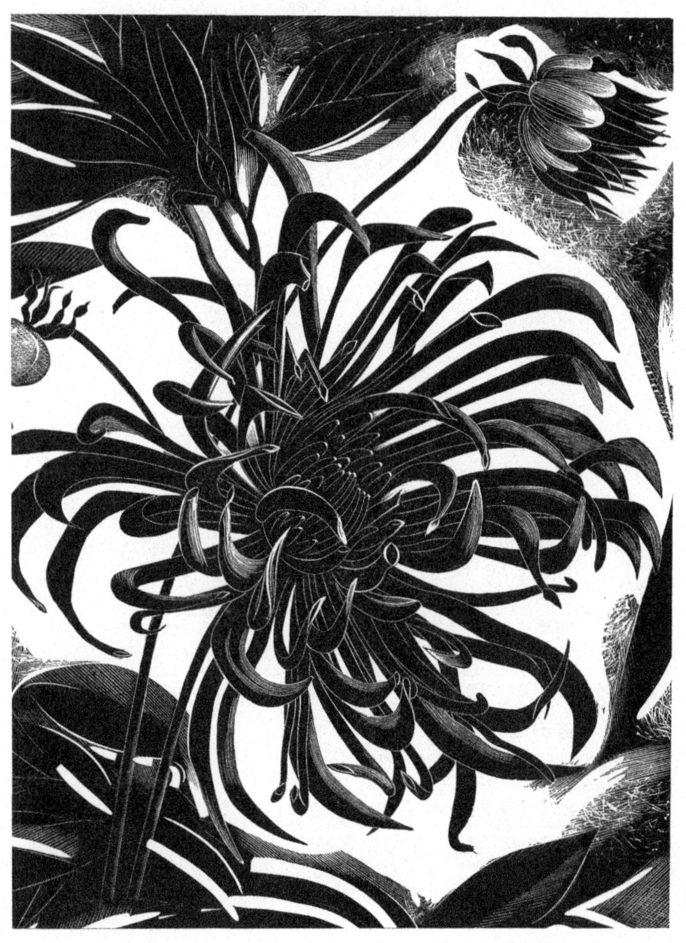

DOVER PUBLICATIONS
GARDEN CITY, NEW YORK

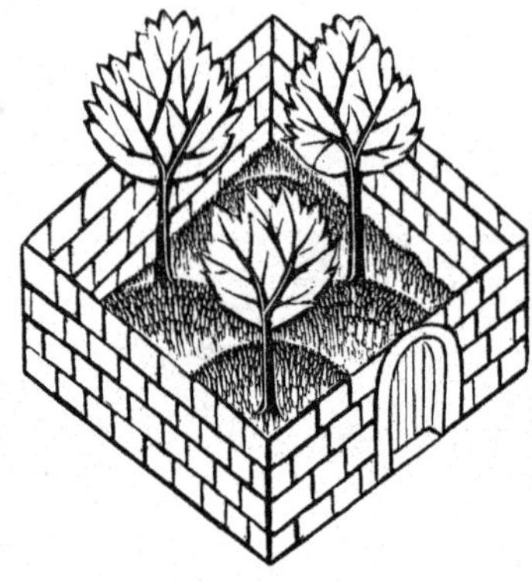

ERIC GILL: A Garden enclosed

This Dover edition, first published in 2015, is an unabridged republication of the work originally published by Art and Technics, Ltd., London, in 1951. This collection of wood-engravings, with Thomas Balston's essay, was first published in November 1950 as a special issue (number 5) of the quarterly *Image.*

Library of Congress Cataloging-in-Publication Data

Balston, Thomas.
English wood-engraving 1900–1950 / Thomas Balston.
pages cm
Includes bibliographical references.
ISBN-13: 978-0-486-79878-3 (paperback)
ISBN-10: 0-486-79878-X
1. Wood-engraving, English. I. Title.
NE1144.B34 2015
761'.20942—dc23

2015020475

Manufactured in the United States of America
79878003
www.doverpublications.com

INTRODUCTION

FROM THE death of Bewick in 1828 till nearly the end of the nineteenth century, the art of original wood-engraving was dormant in England; all the skill of the craftsmen was employed on the reproduction of works of artists who had little or no interest in the medium. But the period covered by this book, 1900–1950, saw the rise of the now flourishing school of artist-craftsmen whose works are so fundamentally different in design and technique from anything which preceded them as to constitute a new branch of the art.

Much of this work has appeared in books, and is now familiar to a host of readers, thousands of whom had the opportunity of appreciating its variety and beauty at the exhibition, *Wood-Engraving in Modern English Books*, held by the National Book League in the autumn of 1949. But that exhibition, as its title showed, could not include any of the immense number of independent wood-engravings made by British artists during this half-century. Such engravings are often the most characteristic and ambitious of an artist's works because he has complete freedom in choosing their subjects, their sizes and their colour, but, as they are generally published in small limited editions, and can seldom be seen except at temporary exhibitions, they are much less well-known to the public. In this book, therefore, though it covers both these branches of the art, the illustrations have been selected with some bias in favour of the less familiar class.

Among the illustrations will be found eight examples of coloured wood-engraving, a branch of the art which has made great strides of recent years. There are also three examples of the work of Edward Wadsworth, which, though woodcuts and not wood-engravings, had so marked an influence on the work of some engravers that the book would have been incomplete without them.

Though my name appears alone upon the title-page, I must acknowledge a debt to Mr Robert Harling, who asked me to undertake this task, and, with the able assistance of Miss Clare Blanshard, collected hundreds of excellent engravings. From them he selected those which could be most satisfactorily printed by machine. In this selection he bound himself by one invaluable rule, viz. that no engraving should be reproduced except on its original scale. In a few cases, where an engraving of conspicuous merit proved too large for the page, small marginal areas have been omitted, always with the artist's approval.

I must also express my gratitude to the National Book League for very kindly permitting me to repeat those passages in my *Introduction* to their *Catalogue* which are relevant to the present wider subject-matter.

T. B.

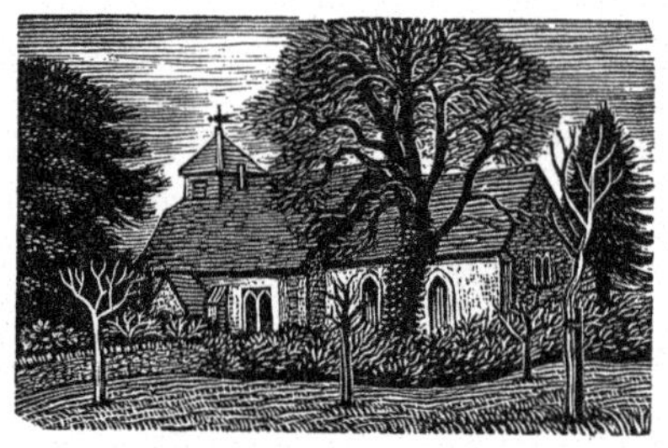

REYNOLDS STONE

CONTENTS

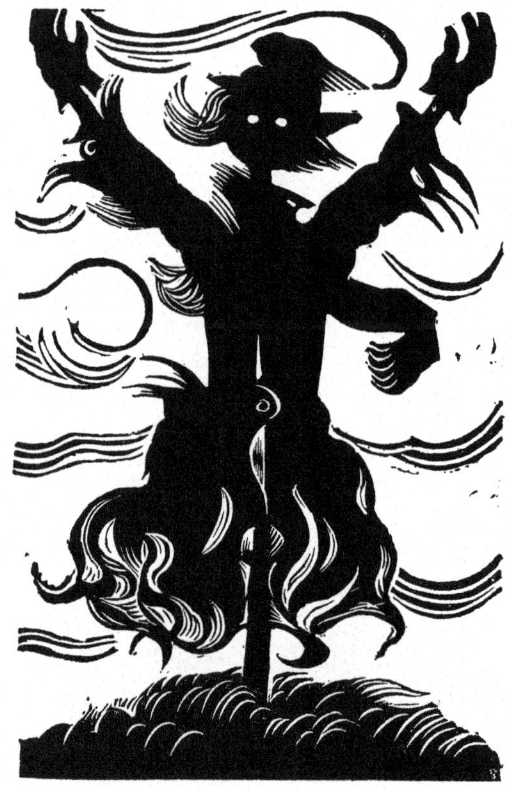

DOUGLAS PERCY BLISS: Device for Shenval Press

THE ENGRAVERS

[*The italic page numbers are the illustrations*]

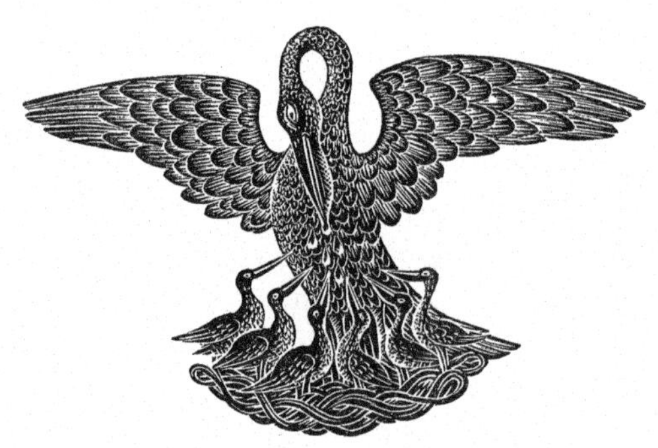

ERIC GILL

ENGLISH WOOD-ENGRAVING
1900-1950

THE YEARS BEFORE

THE WORD 'WOODCUT' is commonly used to denote two different things, the woodcut proper and the wood-engraving. They agree, however, in being printed from the surface of the block (a print from a wood block before any work has been done on it would be a black rectangle the size of the block), unlike copper-engravings, which are printed, after the surface has been wiped clean, by pressing the paper into the incised lines into which the ink has been forced.[1]

The woodcut preceded the wood-engraving by many centuries. It was first employed in western Europe to print patterns on textiles. The designs were made on the block by slanting cuts with a knife, so that two cuts more or less parallel could make a V-shaped trench which printed as a white line, like a chalk-line drawn on a blackboard, while the rest of the surface of the block printed black. But when the invention of movable type in the fifteenth century gave rise to a demand for woodcuts to be printed with letterpress, the wooden presses of the period were found too weak to print the large areas of black efficiently. The woodcutters therefore adopted a new technique. Instead of making their designs of white lines on black, they cut away the wood on both sides of lines already drawn upon the block, and removed all bare areas of the surface with a gouge. These lines then printed black, and the

[1] Eric Gill from 1924 onwards experimented with intaglio printing (i.e. as from copper-plates) from engraved wood blocks. He contributed an article on the subject to Herbert Furst's *The Woodcut: An Annual*, vol. I (1927).

rest of the block white. All illustrations were soon made in black line only, and worked on the side-grain or plank of some soft wood so as to lessen the labour of the cutting and gouging. Printer-publishers then found it cheaper to employ an artist only to draw on the block and then get a craftsman to do all the cutting and gouging. Thus woodcutting was degraded to a purely reproductive craft.

So, for a hundred years, innumerable black-line woodcuts appeared in books and single sheets, but about the middle of the sixteenth century they were superseded in all the more important books by copper-engravings. Copper-engravings, however, entail much greater expense because the plates, not being printed from the surface, cannot be printed in the same operation as type. Hence towards the end of the seventeenth century attempts were made to imitate copper-engravings on wood blocks and, as the crisp and often very fine lines on the copper-plates could not be satisfactorily imitated on a soft plank, the experiment was tried of working with a graver on the end grain of a hard wood such as box. Thus wood-engraving was born, but another century elapsed before, in Bewick's hands, it developed into an original art.

The first English book known to have been decorated with wood-engravings is Howell's *Medulla Historiae Anglicanae* (1712), in which, as the Bookseller's Preface states, the plates were engraved on wood because 'copper would be more beautiful but more expensive', and the wood-engravers soon became so skilful in imitating copper that it is still disputed whether some prints of the period, e.g. those in Croxall's *Fables* (1722), were from wood or metal. In 1775, when the Society of Arts offered a prize for 'the best engraving on wood or type capable of being worked off with letterpress', it was won by a young engraver from Newcastle-on-Tyne, Thomas Bewick (1753–1828), with five wood-engravings based on prints in Croxall's book.

Stimulated by this success, Bewick continued to engrave on wood, but abandoned the attempt to imitate the black lines of copper-engravings. Though not, as has been frequently asserted, the inventor of wood-engraving, he was the first to recognize that, as the incisions made by the graver on the wood block printed white, the right use of the medium was to base his designs as much as possible on white lines and areas, and so he became the first to use his graver as a drawing instrument and to employ the medium as an original art. He seldom drew pen or pencil lines on the block, but generally worked from water-colour sketches, whose tones and textures he freely interpreted with small pits and jags from his graver. Because his main interest was in the exact rendering on a very small scale of all the details of birds and animals and country scenes, he did not employ the long and narrow white lines which are a conspicuous feature of many modern engravings. His own claim was that he was the first 'to attempt colour on wood', and by colour he meant tone, the rendering of light.

Bewick, however, was a sensitive rather than an inventive artist: 'he could draw,' said Ruskin, 'a pig but not an Aphrodite': and it was his preoccupation with the exact rendering of natural objects which quickly led to the eclipse of wood-engraving as an independent art. The publishers were not slow to grasp that craftsmen as highly trained as Bewick's apprentices to copy natural objects would be equally skilful in reproducing the drawings of other artists. Very soon the craftsmen found that this was the only remunerative work they could obtain, and wood-engraving, for nearly eighty years, became a merely reproductive craft, just as woodcutting had done three centuries earlier. Three men, it is true, employed Bewick's technique on a few very original and imaginative designs of their own, but Blake's and Calvert's and Samuel Palmer's prints aroused little public interest at the time and created no demand for original work.

This eclipse of original wood-engraving would be entirely deplorable if it had not given rise to the famous engravings of the 'sixties in which, with amazing ingenuity, the craftsmen set themselves to make facsimiles of the drawings of Millais, Leighton, Rossetti, Holman Hunt, Keene, Tenniel, Houghton, Pinwell, and a host of others, the greatest school of popular illustrators that has existed in England. Though much of the sensitiveness of their lines was lost in translation in spite of the virtuosity of the craftsmen, their illustrations to books and magazines and weekly papers retained the enthusiastic interest of a large public for more than twenty years, and only lost their vogue in the middle 'eighties when the publishers transferred their allegiance to the photographic line-block, a much quicker and cheaper process for reproducing drawings.

For many years not only wood-engraving but copper-engraving and etching had been esteemed only as means of reproducing drawings and paintings, and it was an etcher, Sir Seymour Haden, who, in a paper read before the Society of Arts in 1883, made the first effective protest in favour of original work. Six years later two young artists, Charles Ricketts and Charles Shannon, inspired by the principles, though not the practice, of William Morris, made a similar protest in favour of original woodcutting and wood-engraving. Between 1889 and 1897 they published, at very irregular intervals, five numbers of a new magazine, *The Dial*, which contained wood-engravings designed and cut by themselves, Sturge Moore, Reginald Savage, and Lucien Pissarro, and two books with many woodcuts by themselves alone, *Daphnis and Chloe* (1893) and *Hero and Leander* (1894). Further work by all five can be found in many volumes of the Vale Press (1896–1904) and the Eragny Press (1894–1914). In 1898, as the Vale Press Group, they staged what they claimed to be 'the first exhibition of original wood-engraving' in this country, but the exhibits, however beautiful in themselves, were not in any true sense original engravings. They were still essentially copies of drawings although, as the same hand generally drew on the block and engraved it, the drawings were better suited to this method of reproduction than those of the 'sixties. In some works, it is true, Ricketts and Pissarro employed white line in their backgrounds, and in some Pissarro employed black line which made no attempt to imitate the calligraphic effect of pen or pencil, but even these were mainly reproductive.

There were, however, two men in the 'nineties who, quietly and with no propaganda, were really designing *in* and not *on* the wood. About 1892 William Nicholson, inspired by Joseph Crawhall's imitations of old chapbooks, began to engrave those simple designs with heavy black masses which, when enlivened by a lithographic buff tone and some touches of local colour, became famous, first in his *Twelve Portraits* (which included the Queen Victoria) and later in *London Types* and other volumes published between 1898 and 1902. It is a fair comment that these designs might more easily have been cut with a knife on soft wood, but those of his pupil in the craft, Gordon Craig, are thoroughbred engravings. Craig's finest work belongs to the next decades, but from 1895 to 1900 he produced more than 150 engravings, mostly slight but remarkable for the originality of his designs and for the varied technique employed in their execution.

THE NEW MOVEMENT

1900–1920

IN 1900, when our period opens, and for the next twenty years, there was little public interest in wood-engraving. Nicholson and the Vale Press Group, with the exception of Pissarro, had already done their most distinguished work, and Pissarro's Eragny Press books, in which his new engravings continued to appear till 1914, did not at that time arouse the interest which was due to them, especially for the splendour and harmony of his colour prints. Craig, too, continued to engrave, and started to cut with the knife, but even now his masterpieces, the theatrical woodcuts which he made in Florence between 1900 and 1914, including the *Hamlet* and *Merchant of Venice* series, are almost unknown in England.

It was, however, early in this period that the seeds were sown of a revival of the wood block which was, at the end of the First War, to make original wood-engraving more widely appreciated than ever before. The early history of the 'modern' movement is as obscure and complicated as that of most developments in the arts, but its main thread derives from some date in 1904 when Noel Rooke became so much dissatisfied with the reproductions of his drawings by photographic process that after much discussion with Edward Johnston he turned to wood-engraving. Soon, however, he perceived that the wood block, too, was only a very distorting medium for reproducing pen and pencil drawings, and that a wood-engraving could only have the quality of an original work of art if it was designed by the artist, graver in hand, with incisions dictated by the medium itself and not by the quite alien pen or pencil. Thereupon he sought the advice of Pissarro, who helped him in various ways but could not sympathize with his enthusiasm for a graver-designed technique. Eric Gill, however, who had been Rooke's fellow student under Johnston, warmly welcomed the idea. During the next ten years Gill engraved some letters, designed by himself or Johnston, and a number of small devices, Christmas cards and bookplates, and Rooke, too, made a number of engravings. In 1905 he had been appointed Teacher of Book Illustration at the Central School of Arts and Crafts, and in 1912, in spite of much opposition, he was permitted to instruct his students in wood-engraving. Among the first were Vivien Gribble, Rachel Marshall (Mrs David Garnett), and Robert Gibbings. Rooke later became Head of the School of Book Production at the Central School, and for thirty years continued to teach wood-engraving as a medium for the decoration of books.

Meanwhile, independently of Rooke, Gwendolen Raverat, then a student at the Slade School, had been inspired by admiration for Bewick to start wood-engraving. At that time no one at the Slade had the slightest interest in the craft, but she had the luck to obtain some instruction from her cousin, Eleanor Monsell (Mrs Bernard Darwin), who had begun to cut and engrave wood blocks as early as 1898 but soon desisted owing to the pressure of other work. By 1914 Mrs Raverat had nearly sixty blocks to her credit. Some of them, especially a few designed or inspired by her husband, have been said to show the influence of Gill, but at that period she was unacquainted with Gill's work.

Side by side with this revival of original wood-engraving there was some revival of original woodcutting. In these years before the First War, Rooke himself made some side-grain cuts, and was probably the first to experiment with the side-grain of boxwood instead of the softer woods generally employed. But his attempts to instruct his pupils in woodcutting had little result, as the pupils all showed a marked preference for engraving although many of the early designs of Gibbings and others were stark juxtapositions of black and white masses which could have been more directly executed by the knife. But there was one independent artist, Edward Wadsworth, who realized that the woodcut was the right medium for his bold and much simplified renderings of natural objects. An early work of his, *Newcastle-on-Tyne*, was printed in Wyndham Lewis' magazine, *Blast* (June 1914), and during the next five years he produced many prints of marked originality. His series of camouflaged ships were among the first modernist works to attract wide notice and, though cut with the knife, had a marked influence on the designs of many contemporary engravers.

By 1915 only a few prints in magazines, handbills and so on had given the public a glimpse of this new kind of art, but in that year there were published two slim volumes which were the first to be illustrated by modern wood-engravings: *The Devil's Devices* (Hampshire House

Workshops) illustrated by Gill, and *Spring Morning* (Poetry Bookshop) by Mrs Raverat. In the following year the St Dominic's Press began to issue its many little pamphlets decorated by Gill and his pupils. None of these, coming as they did from obscure publishers, attracted much attention at the time, but the cult of the wood block was spreading among the younger artists and, when the war ended, it was found that many of them were acquiring the craft. In 1919 a little magazine, *Change*, edited by John Hilton and Joseph Thorp, of which only two numbers appeared, gave some prominence to the work of nine engravers, among whom were Gill, Gibbings and Vivien Gribble, and, in its January number, *The Studio* published an appreciation of Gibbings' work, its first article on a modern wood-engraver.

The next year, 1920, was marked by a more important advance, the foundation of the Society of Wood-Engravers to further the interests of those who, whether working in black or in colours, with knife or with graver, used the European method of printing with oil-based inks.[1] There were ten original members, of whom seven—Rooke, Gibbings, Gill, Mrs Raverat, John Nash, Philip Hagreen, and E. M. O'R. Dickey—were definitely of the modern movement. The other three were Pissarro who, as we have seen, was in incomplete sympathy with Rooke's aims, Gordon Craig whose work is too individual to be considered as part of any movement, and Sydney Lee who, from about 1905, had been making a few engravings of distinction in the modern manner but was more intent on cuts, black or coloured, in the Japanese tradition. In November the Society held its first Annual Exhibition at the Chenil Gallery in King's Road, Chelsea, with a catalogue introduced by Dr Campbell Dodgson of the British Museum. Of the ninety works exhibited seventy-nine were by the members: among the non-members

[1] About the same time the Colour Woodcut Society was formed for those who, under the leadership of F. Morley Fletcher, J. D. Batten, and William Giles, worked in the Japanese tradition, and printed their cuts with rice-paste and water.

exhibiting were Ethelbert White, E. F. Daglish, Rupert Lee, Desmond Chute, and Margaret Pilkington.

Of the engravers not previously mentioned Chute and Hagreen had learnt their craft from Gill, Margaret Pilkington from Rooke, and Rupert Lee from Gibbings. White was self-taught, and John Nash and Dickey had started under the aegis of Paul Nash who, fired perhaps by the example of his then neighbour, Rupert Lee, had begun to experiment with the medium in 1918, though he did not exhibit with the Society till its second exhibition in 1921.

Two of the leaders, Rooke and Gill, were primarily interested in engraving in relation to letterpress, and even before the first exhibition some big commercial houses had discovered how effective the new engravings could be as decorations of their advertisements and, for a short period which ended with the first post-war financial slump in the summer of 1921, paid high prices to a few of the artists. But none of the regular book-publishers had yet commissioned such work, with the result that most of the exhibits were independent engravings in which the artist's vision was untrammelled by any text or by the necessity of accommodating the size and colour of his design to letterpress.

Partly in reaction against the grey and lifeless prints of the reproductive engravers of the 'eighties and 'nineties, and partly because the engravers had not yet learnt all the technical devices by which black masses can be broken up with a pleasing variety of tone and texture, many of their works contained broad masses of black and white too powerful to balance against any type easily legible by modern eyes. Some of them, however, in which the artist had accommodated his design to his limited technical resources, were so striking that, in his foreword to the catalogue of the second exhibition, Dr Dodgson declared that they would 'make, when framed, an excellent effect in the decoration of small rooms such as most of the world inhabits in days when the burden of taxes is heavy'. Many others were of this opinion, and the artists were given much encouragement, if not a livelihood, by sales of individual prints until this market was almost killed by the slump of 1930.

Most of the contributors to this and the subsequent annual exhibitions of the Society of Wood-Engravers were more interested in design than in representation, and therefore employed the medium so differently from Bewick, either by the use of broader masses of black and white or by longer and narrower lines, that they created what was essentially a new art, and in this new art, owing to their comparative independence of tradition or of any central influence, produced works of remarkable variety. Visitors were surprised and delighted by many designs of a kind which they had never seen before, ranging from Gill's hieratic silhouettes, relieved by the most delicate white lines, to the stark contrasts of black and white areas in Gibbings' designs from Mediterranean architecture. And among the visitors were some publishers who were inspired to give commissions for book-illustrations without which the new art would have been starved, and these led to the publication of such original works as Paul Nash's *Places* (Heinemann 1922), Vivien Gribble's *Sixe Idillia of Theocritus* (Duckworth 1922), and Ethelbert White's *The Story of My Heart* (Duckworth 1923).

The support of the general publisher, however, was for many years to prove less important to the movement than the rise of the Golden Cockerel Press. Founded in 1921 to print 'new works of literary significance by young authors', it had published seventeen books, of which only one contained wood-engravings, before, early in 1924, it was taken over by Gibbings, and started on that specialization in books with wood-engravings which has made it famous. For nine years under Gibbings, and ever since under Christopher Sandford, it has given employment to nearly all the chief engravers of the period. The Gregynog Press, too, founded in 1922, concentrated on books with wood-engravings by its first Director, R. A. Maynard, who had taught himself to engrave, and his pupil, H. W. Bray. Except for one Welsh book illustrated by David Jones, who had started engraving under Gill in 1922, the Press employed no other artists until 1931, when it came under new management.

EXPERIMENTS

1921–1924

THE ARTISTS who exhibited at the first exhibition, with the one addition of Paul Nash, must be considered the pioneers of the movement, but hosts of others had already begun, or very soon began, to experiment with the craft. At the second exhibition there were seventeen new names among the contributors, and further recruits at all the subsequent shows. Many of these either did not persevere, or never achieved any great distinction in the medium, but among them were some who ultimately contributed much to the success of the movement.

Eric Ravilious and Douglas Percy Bliss became students at the Royal College of Art in 1921. Sir Frank Short, then Professor of Engraving, set little store by wood-engraving, but Paul Nash was teaching Design. Inspired by some of Nash's engravings on the College walls, and with much encouragement from him, they picked up the craft for themselves, and in 1926, with the publication of Ravilious' *Desert* and Bliss' *Rasselas*, became recognized as excellent craftsmen and designers. In 1921, too, Hughes-Stanton, Gertrude Hermes and Mary Groom joined Leon Underwood's School and, roused by the enthusiasm of an American fellow-student, Marion Mitchell, who had been taught by Gibbings, tried their own hands at the craft. Encouraged by Underwood, who soon began to practise the craft himself, and inspired by his sense of design and, like Bliss and Ravilious, by the engravings of Paul Nash, they soon formed a very distinct group in the movement. At first they exhibited with the Society of Wood-Engravers, but when it appeared that their innovations in design and technique, especially their use of the multiple tool which Mary Groom had brought from France, were not very sympathetically received by some of the older members, they seceded, and in 1925 founded the English Wood-Engraving Society, which held annual exhibitions at the St George's Gallery in George Street, Hanover Square.

There was, however, no hard and fast boundary between the two societies, many artists exhibiting at both, and so in 1932, when the great slump had seriously impaired the market for prints, the new society comfortably coalesced with the old.

For some years the Underwood group had concentrated on independent engravings, but in 1928 the twelve plates engraved by Hughes-Stanton and Gertrude Hermes for the Cresset Press' monumental edition of *The Pilgrim's Progress* printed by the Shakespeare's Head Press gave conclusive evidence of their ability to work with letterpress. Three years later Hughes-Stanton succeeded Maynard at the Gregynog Press, and there illustrated *The Revelation of St John* (1932) and six other books.

Others who started in 1921 or soon after were Claughton Pellew and Clifford Webb. Pellew, under the inspiration of John Nash, and Webb, who taught himself, soon won recognition by their independent prints, though more lately, from 1937 onwards, Webb has done work of great distinction for the Golden Cockerel Press. Clare Leighton and Farleigh, too, both pupils of Rooke and following their master's precepts, worked with letterpress almost from the start, and became the first original wood-engravers for nearly a hundred years to achieve popularity with the general reading public. Farleigh, indeed, began with the Golden Cockerel and Shakespeare's Head Presses, to both of which he was introduced by Rooke, but it was his illustrations to an unlimited edition, Bernard Shaw's *The Adventures of the Black Girl*, published by Constable in 1932, and especially his design for its cover, that won him wide appreciation. Nearly all his later work on wood blocks has been done for general publishers, though he has made some distinguished independent prints. Clare Leighton is unique among these engravers in having made her name independently of the Private Presses.

THE YEARS OF SUCCESS

1925–1939

ALL THE ARTISTS yet mentioned had started before the new art had established itself with the booksellers. Down to the end of 1924 the Private Press books had been slight and the only substantial work with wood-engravings issued by a general publisher had been Richard Jefferies' *Story of My Heart* (Duckworth 1923) with thirty-six engravings by Ethelbert White. In the next six or seven years little progress was made with the general publishers, though Dent's edition of Dr Johnson's *Rasselas* (1926), with twenty engravings by Bliss, was a notable exception, but the Private Presses, especially the Golden Cockerel, produced many works of great importance, culminating in the Golden Cockerel's *The Four Gospels* (1931). Few collaborations of artist and typographer have been more successful than that of Gill and Gibbings in this magnificent quarto, set in Gill's Golden Cockerel type, and decorated with forty-one of his engravings.

During these years there were further notable recruits. In 1925 John Buckland-Wright was inspired by Gordon Craig's *Woodcuts and Some Words* (Dent 1924) to teach himself the craft, and during the next ten years illustrated many books in Belgium, France and Holland, though it was not till 1936 that he did the first of his many books for the Golden Cockerel, *Love Night* by Powys Mathers. About 1925, too, Tirzah Garwood (later Mrs Eric Ravilious) had lessons from Ravilious at the Eastbourne School of Art, and for some years made engravings with a very individual humour and technique, but never illustrated a book. Agnes Miller-Parker, on the other hand, who began to teach herself in 1926, soon became known for her illustrations, very original in design and texture, to *The Fables of Esope*, published by the Gregynog Press in 1931. Since then she has illustrated many books, mostly for general publishers: among them are five volumes of Richard Jefferies' works.

A source of valuable recruits at this period was the Grosvenor School of Art, founded by Iain Macnab in 1925. He himself began to exhibit engravings as early as 1927, and among his pupils in the next few years were Peter Barker-Mill, who has exhibited no independent prints, but has illustrated Bligh's *Voyage in the Resource* (1937) and other books for the Golden Cockerel with very imaginative and skilful engravings, Gwenda Morgan, who has done three books for the same Press, and Averil and Winifred Mackenzie, both of whom have exhibited large and powerful independent prints. Averil has also illustrated books for the Golden Cockerel.

Another recruit of this period was William Armour who, about 1930, taught himself by studying Beedham's *Wood-Engraving* and other handbooks, and began to exhibit independent prints in 1934.

In the last years before the Second War, owing perhaps to the success of Farleigh's *Adventures of the Black Girl* published in December 1932, there was a great increase in the number of unlimited editions with wood-engravings issued by general publishers. In 1934 Black published Farleigh's *Story of David*, Faber Mrs Raverat's *Farmer's Glory*, Maclehose Bliss' *The Devil in Scotland*, and Dent volumes of his *New Temple Shakespeare* with engravings by Gill. Thereafter these and other publishers commissioned many works, especially from the three chief women engravers, Mrs Raverat, Agnes Miller-Parker and Clare Leighton. A fourth, Joan Hassall, a pupil of R. J. Beedham, joined them in 1936 with a frontispiece to *Devil's Dyke* (Heinemann), but it was not till the war that, with her illustrations to *Cranford* (Harrap

1940), somewhat in the vein of the pen-and-ink illustrators of the 'nineties, she became known to a large and appreciative public.

There were other recruits, too, who made their names before the war. Reynolds Stone, while a printing apprentice at the University Press, Cambridge, had had the good fortune to receive a fortnight's tuition from Gill, started as an independent engraver in 1934, and decorated his first book *A Butler's Recipe Book* (Cambridge) in 1936. He also became widely known for his engraved letterings for book-plates and letter-headings. C. F. Tunnicliffe, self-taught, made eighty-two engravings for *A Book of Birds* (Gollancz 1937), and has since illustrated other books and made powerful independent engravings of birds and animals. John O'Connor, taught by Ravilious at the Royal College, did his first book for the Golden Cockerel, *Here's Flowers*, in 1937, and Geoffrey Wales, also taught by Ravilious, and by John Nash and Robert Austin, illustrated *The Pilgrim Fathers* for the same house in 1939. And Kingsley Cook, a pupil of Rooke, decorated a Milton's *Comus* printed by the Central School in 1939.

THE WAR AND LATER

WAR, OF COURSE, killed nearly all this enterprise. Most of the engravers were caught up by military service or other war work. For the first three years, at least, there were almost no commissions for bookwork, and for ten years independent engravings lost their best market as the annual exhibitions of the Society of Wood-Engravers were discontinued.

A few books appeared which had been almost completed before the war. Three were published by the Golden Cockerel in the autumn of 1939, and in 1940 Joan Hassall's *Cranford* came from Harrap, and Gibbings' *Sweet Thames, Run Softly* from Dent. This book and its successors, *Coming Down the Wye* (1942) and *Lovely is the Lee* (1944), mark the culmination of Gibbings' progress towards more detailed representation, and to the lighter tone which harmonizes with letterpress by modern machining. All three were printed by the Temple Press, Letchworth, under his supervision, with all the technical skill he had acquired as Director of the Golden Cockerel, and do more justice to the wood blocks than most similar books printed by general printers. Their success was immediate, both here and in America.

Throughout the war the Golden Cockerel, under Christopher Sandford, published further fine books but, with the exception of seven headpieces by Stone to Swinburne's *Lucrezia Borgia* (1942), none of them contained wood-engravings until 1944. Then three appeared, illustrated by Buckland-Wright, Barker-Mill and Dorothea Braby, followed in 1945 by two more, by Dorothea Braby and O'Connor, before the war ended.

Since the war wood-engraving, in spite of the competition of lithography, has re-established much of its position. The Golden Cockerel has employed many engravers, especially those who were little known before the war, and the general publishers have commissioned others. In 1949 the Society of Wood-Engravers again staged an exhibition where the latest independent engravings could be seen, and the National Book League devoted their autumn exhibition to *Wood-Engraving in Modern English Books*. In 1948 the publication of *Wood-Engraving* by George Mackley,[1] who had been Rooke's pupil, provided craftsmen and collectors with a valuable new handbook, and was the first to contain specimens of Mackley's own excellent work.

It is still too early to appraise the work of engravers who have started since the war. One of them, however, Leslie Wood, within a few months of teaching himself the craft, produced work of such quality that he was

[1] Published by the National Magazine Company.

commissioned to illustrate the Cresset Press' edition of *The Adventures of Baron Munchausen* (1948), and another, G. W. Lennox Paterson, now teaching wood-engraving at the Glasgow School of Art, where he himself studied it in the last years before the war, has shown distinguished independent work. More recently, John Worsley, better-known as a naval war artist, has made engravings in a strong realistic manner for the Dropmore Press.

COLOURED WOOD-ENGRAVINGS

THE FIRST MASTER of the coloured wood-engraving, printed from sets of engraved blocks with printers' varnish inks, as opposed to the woodcuts in the Japanese style printed with paste and water, was Lucien Pissarro, who had, as he told Rooke, been chiefly attracted to settle in England by Edmund Evans' reproductive wood-engraving in colour. Before 1900 he had issued two portfolios of wood-engravings, *Twelve Woodcuts in Line and Colours* (1891), of which three were in four colours, and *Travaux des Champs*, of which two were coloured: he had also published a small book, *The Queen of the Fishes* (1894), printed by himself, with five coloured woodcuts in the text. Between 1900 and 1907 six of his Eragny Press books contained one coloured engraving each, the colours becoming progressively more luminous and subtle, but it was not till 1911 that, with the *Livre de Jade*, he gave himself whole-heartedly to colour. This little book, printed on Japanese vellum, its many coloured illustrations and decorations often reinforced with gold, is exquisite in every detail, and is only surpassed by his masterpiece of 1912, *La Charrue d'Erable*, in which the twelve plates, designed by Camille Pissarro, and the thirty illustrations in the text have a variety of colour and texture which can never have been surpassed on wood.

Pissarro remains unequalled in his own *genre*, but some years before 1914 Rooke experimented with coloured engravings and employed on them a process of graduated printing which he borrowed from lithography. Among the first to practise his method was Gibbings, whose *Retreat from Serbia*, *Evening at Gaza*, and *Albert Bridge*, published after the war, were warmly applauded by critics. But as printers' inks are only semi-transparent, especially where one colour is superimposed upon another, these prints had a devitalized appearance, lacking the cleanness of colour and the luminosity which the artists desired. From 1922 onwards the chief engravers of the modern school worked almost entirely in monochrome.

Since 1935, however, there has been a revival of coloured engraving, but without graduated printing. In that year Hughes-Stanton engraved some sets of blocks, and in 1937 Mrs Raverat executed an independent engraving, *The Golden Age*, in four panels, each with four blocks. Two years later she made eight engravings, six with four blocks and two with three, to illustrate *The Bird Talisman*, published by the Cambridge University Press. Since the war Hughes-Stanton, Gertrude Hermes, Clifford Webb and others have fostered the revival, so that coloured engravings became a prominent feature of the Society of Wood-Engravers' exhibition of 1949.

A SELECT BIBLIOGRAPHY CONCERNING ENGLISH WOOD-ENGRAVING

NO CLAIM is made that the select bibliography which follows is definitive or exhaustive. It is a select bibliography, made by the author of these notes, in the belief that any reader or student who can make a fairly intensive reading amongst these books will know all the salient facts in the history and technique of contemporary wood-engraving.

The books range from Douglas Percy Bliss' impressively discursive and scholarly *History of Wood-Engraving* to such modest but necessary monographs upon individual artists as the studies of the work of Eric Ravilious and Robert Gibbings. It is good to know, too, that a small and inexpensive book on the work of Eric Gill by Douglas Cleverdon, who was responsible for the large-scale surveys of that artist's engravings, is also in preparation.

BALSTON, THOMAS
The Wood-Engravings of Robert Gibbings. Art & Technics, 1949

BLISS, DOUGLAS PERCY
A History of Wood-Engraving. Dent, 1928

CLEVERDON, DOUGLAS
The Engravings of Eric Gill. Faber, 1934

CRAIG, EDWARD GORDON
Woodcuts and Some Words. Dent, 1924

DARTON, F. J. H.
Modern Book Illustration in Great Britain and America. The Studio, 1931

DODGSON, CAMPBELL (ed.)
Contemporary English Woodcuts. Duckworth, 1922

FARLEIGH, JOHN
Graven Image. Macmillan, 1940

FURST, HERBERT
The Modern Woodcut. Lane, 1924
The Woodcut, An Annual. 4 vols. The Fleuron, 1927–30

GRAY, BASIL
The English Print. A. & C. Black, 1937

HARLING, ROBERT
Notes on the Wood-Engravings of Eric Ravilious. Faber, 1946

LEIGHTON, CLARE
Wood-Engravings and Woodcuts. The Studio, 1932
Wood-Engravings of the 1930's. The Studio, 1936

MACKLEY, GEORGE
Wood-Engraving. National Magazine Co., 1948

MACNAB, IAIN
The Student's Book of Wood-Engraving. Pitman, 1938

NEWDIGATE, B. H.
The Art of the Book. The Studio, 1938

ROOKE, NOEL
Woodcuts and Wood-Engraving. Print Collectors' Club, 1926

SALAMAN, MALCOLM C.
Modern Woodcuts and Lithographs. The Studio, 1919
British Book Illustration, Yesterday and Today. The Studio, 1923
The Woodcut of Today. The Studio, 1927
The New Woodcut. The Studio, 1930

SLEIGH, BERNARD
Wood-Engraving since 1890. Pitman, 1932

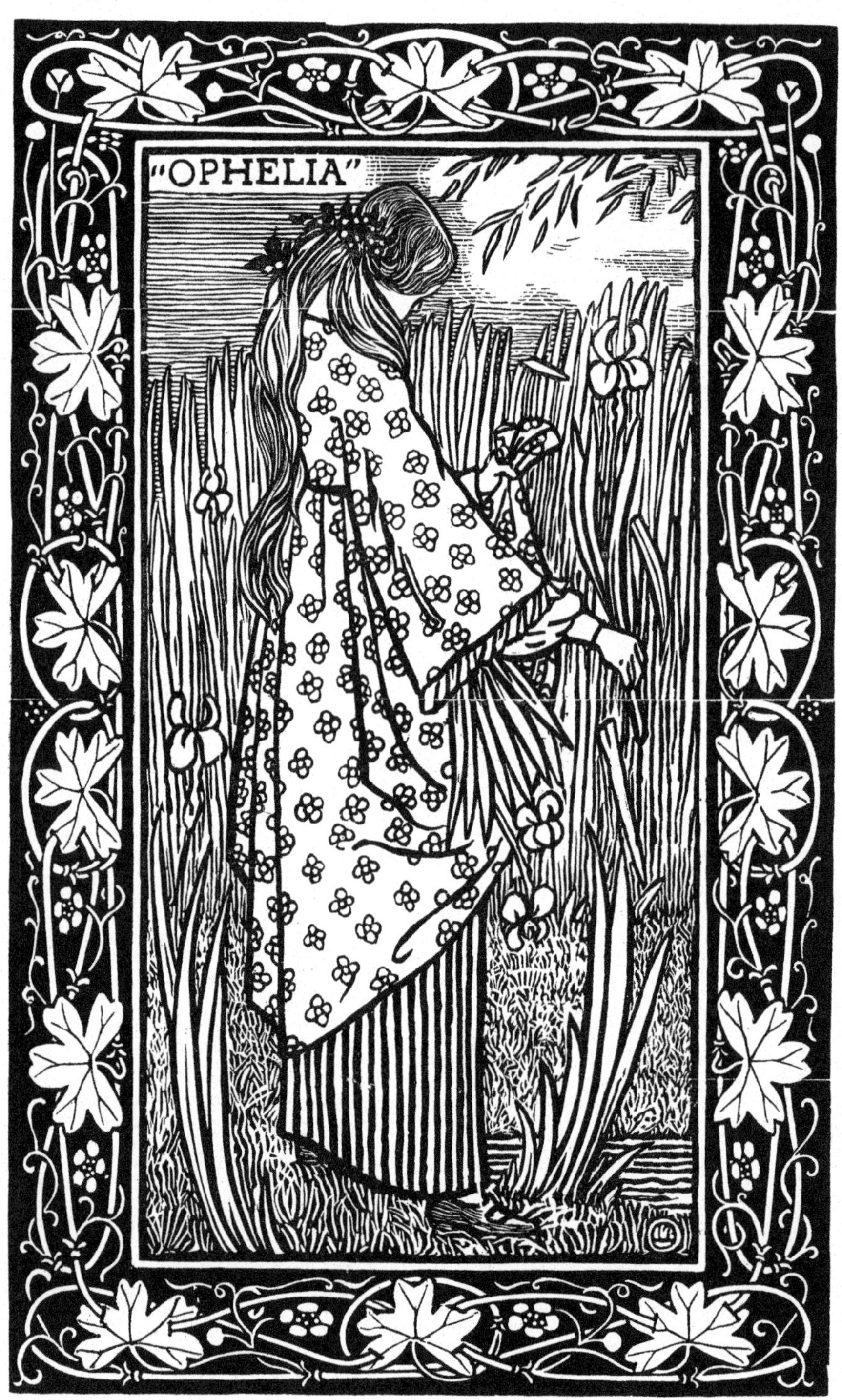

LUCIEN PISSARRO. Frontispiece for *Moralité Legendaires* (Eragny Press, 1898)

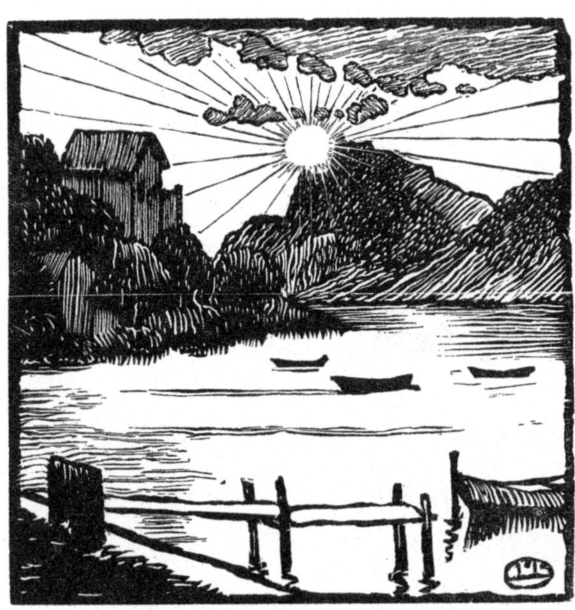

La Pointe de Cargoussa

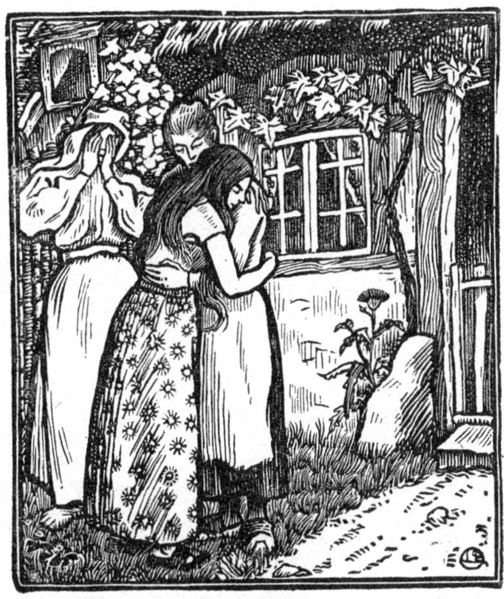

From *The Book of Ruth and the Book of Esther* (Eragny Press, 1896)

LUCIEN PISSARRO

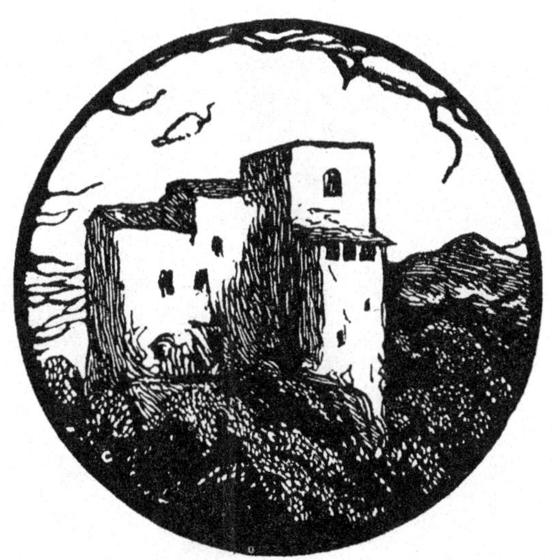

A City, 1907

GORDON CRAIG

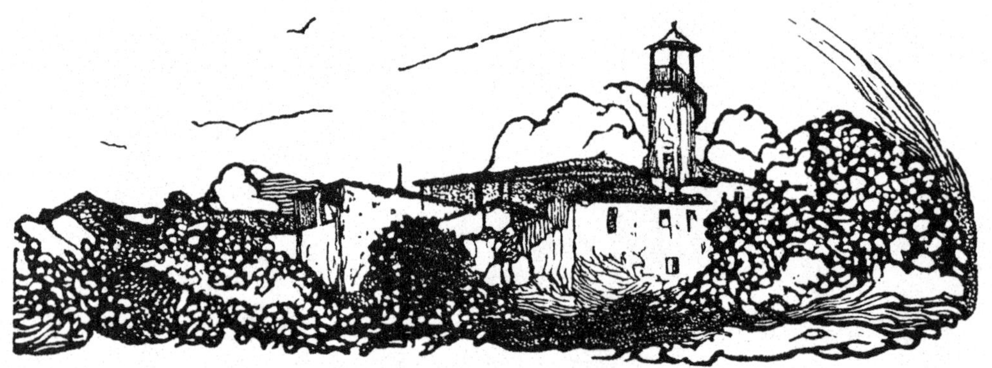

Torre Dei Diavoli, 1908

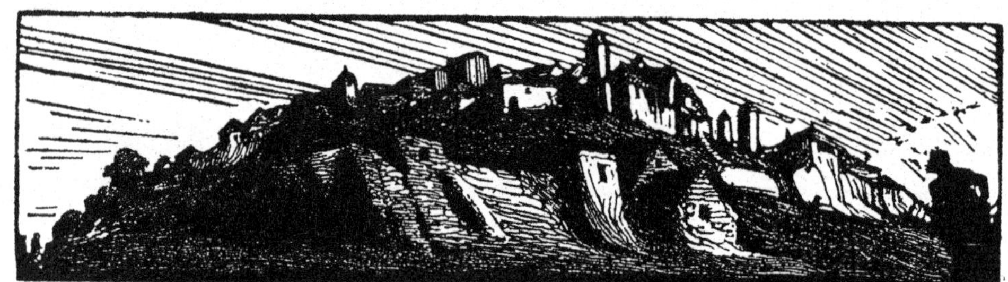

View over Florence, 1908

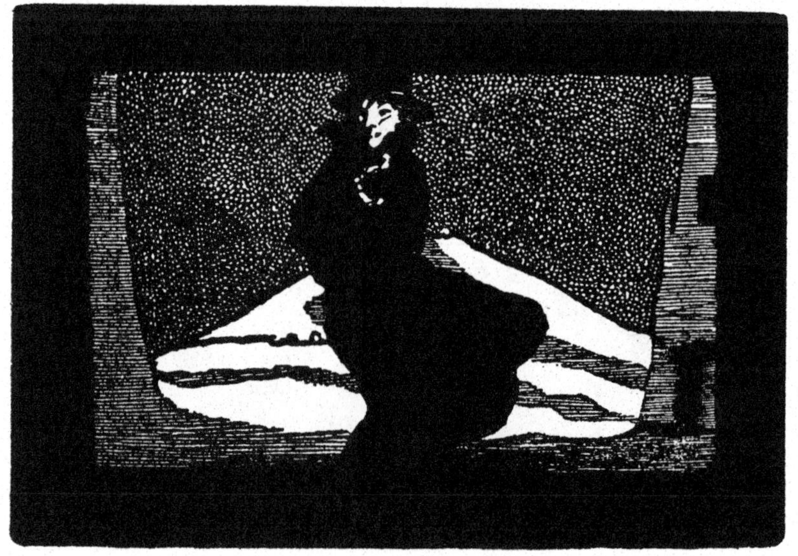

January, 1905

GORDON CRAIG

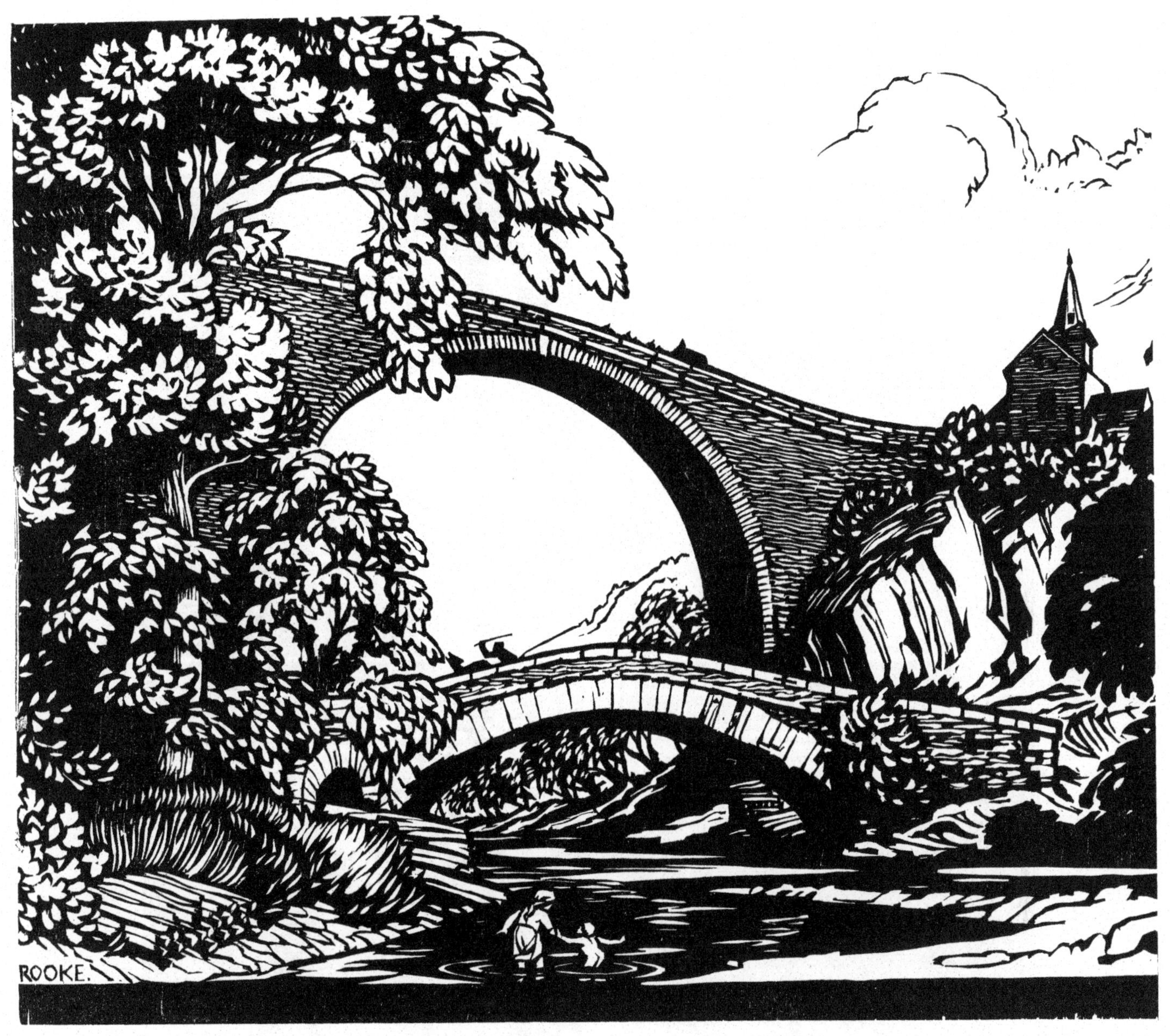

The Two Bridges, 1914

NOEL ROOKE

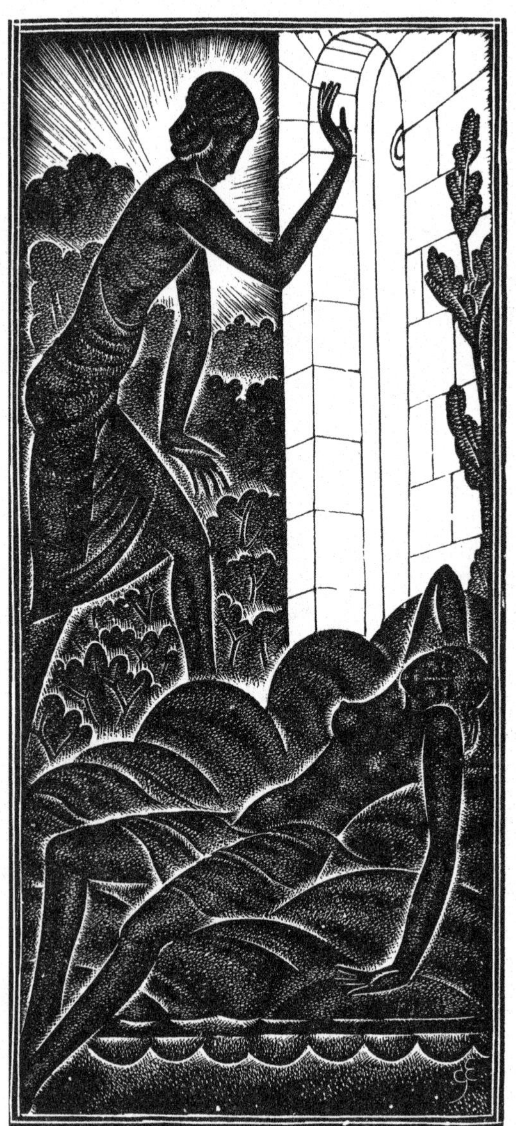

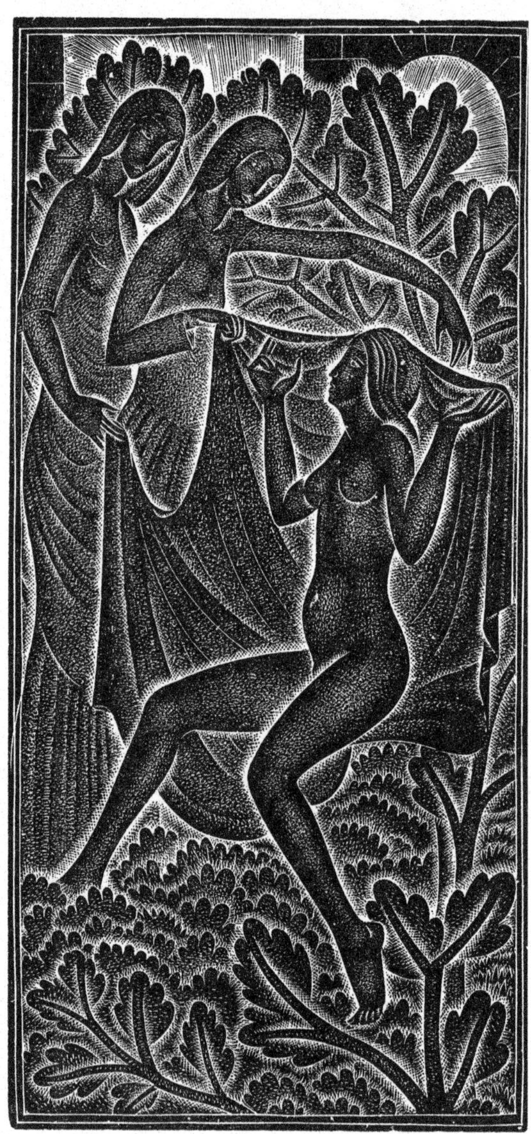

Canticum Canticorum (Cranach Press, Weimar, 1931

ERIC GILL

26

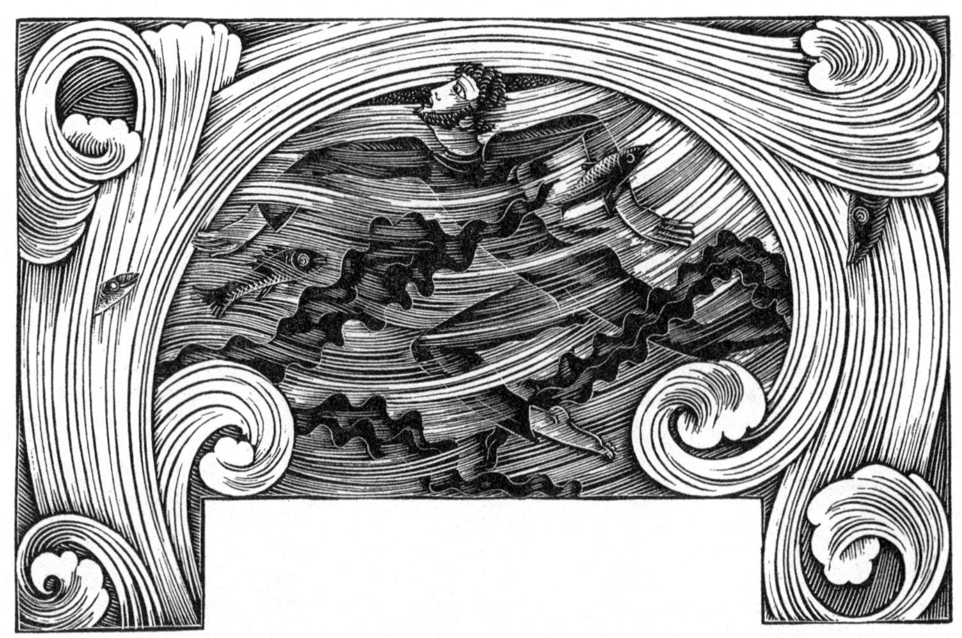

ERIC GILL. Headpiece for *The Green Ship* (Golden Cockerel Press, 1936)

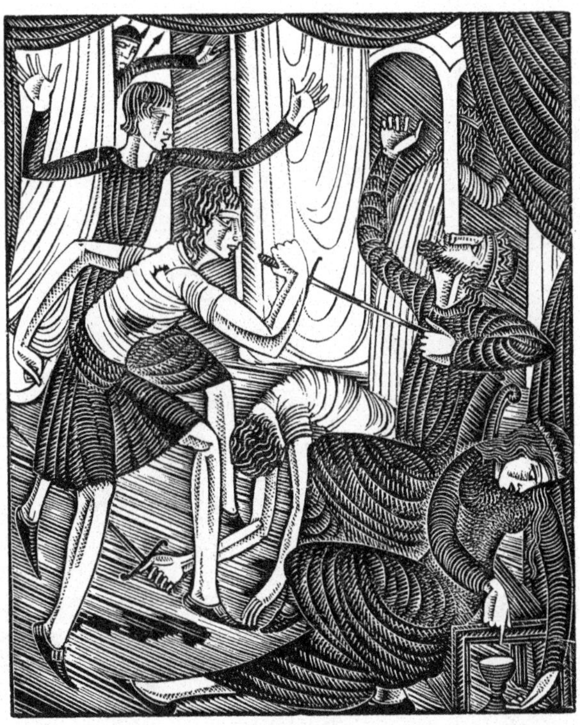

ERIC GILL. *Hamlet, Act V* (Limited Editions Club, New York, 1933)

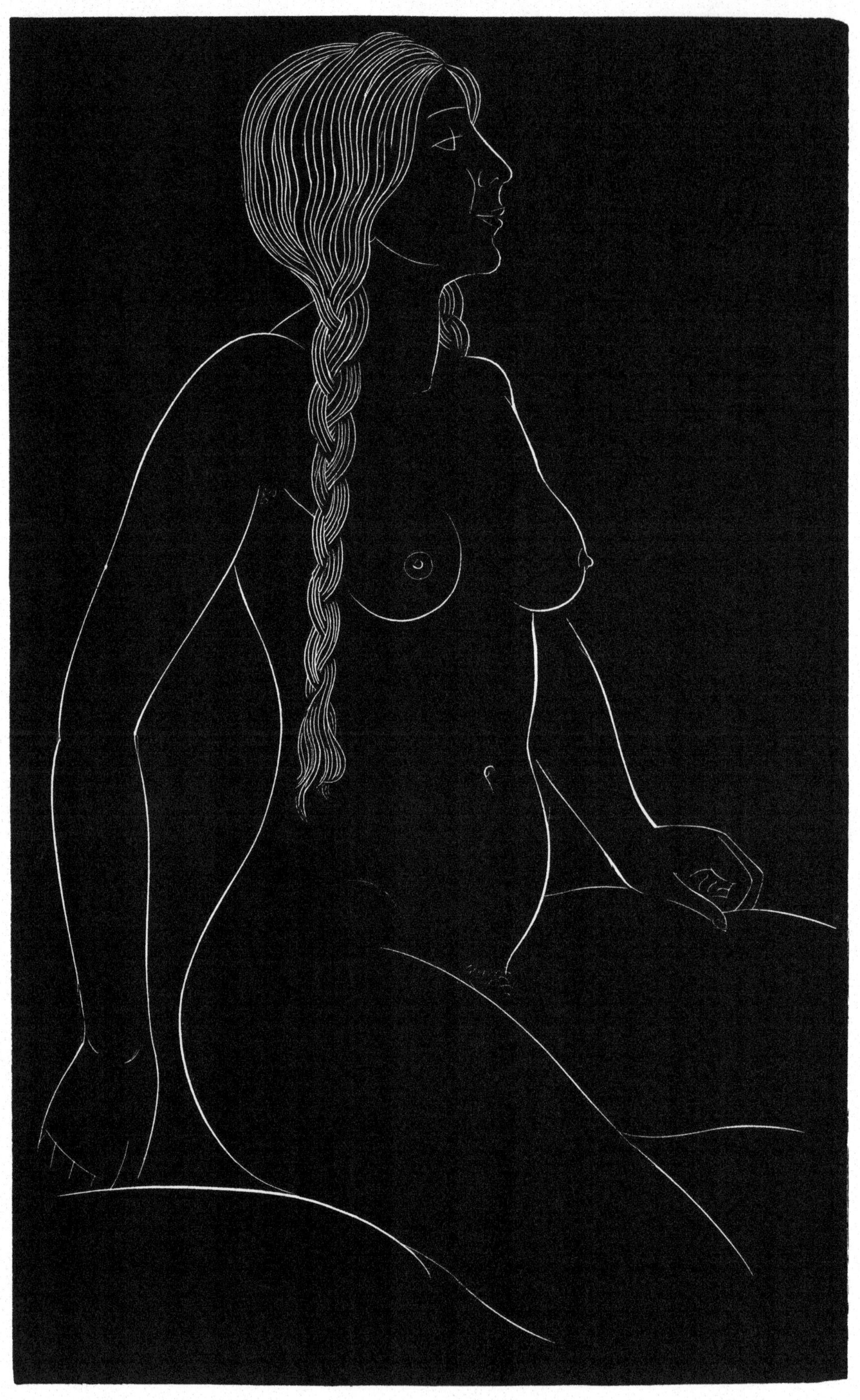

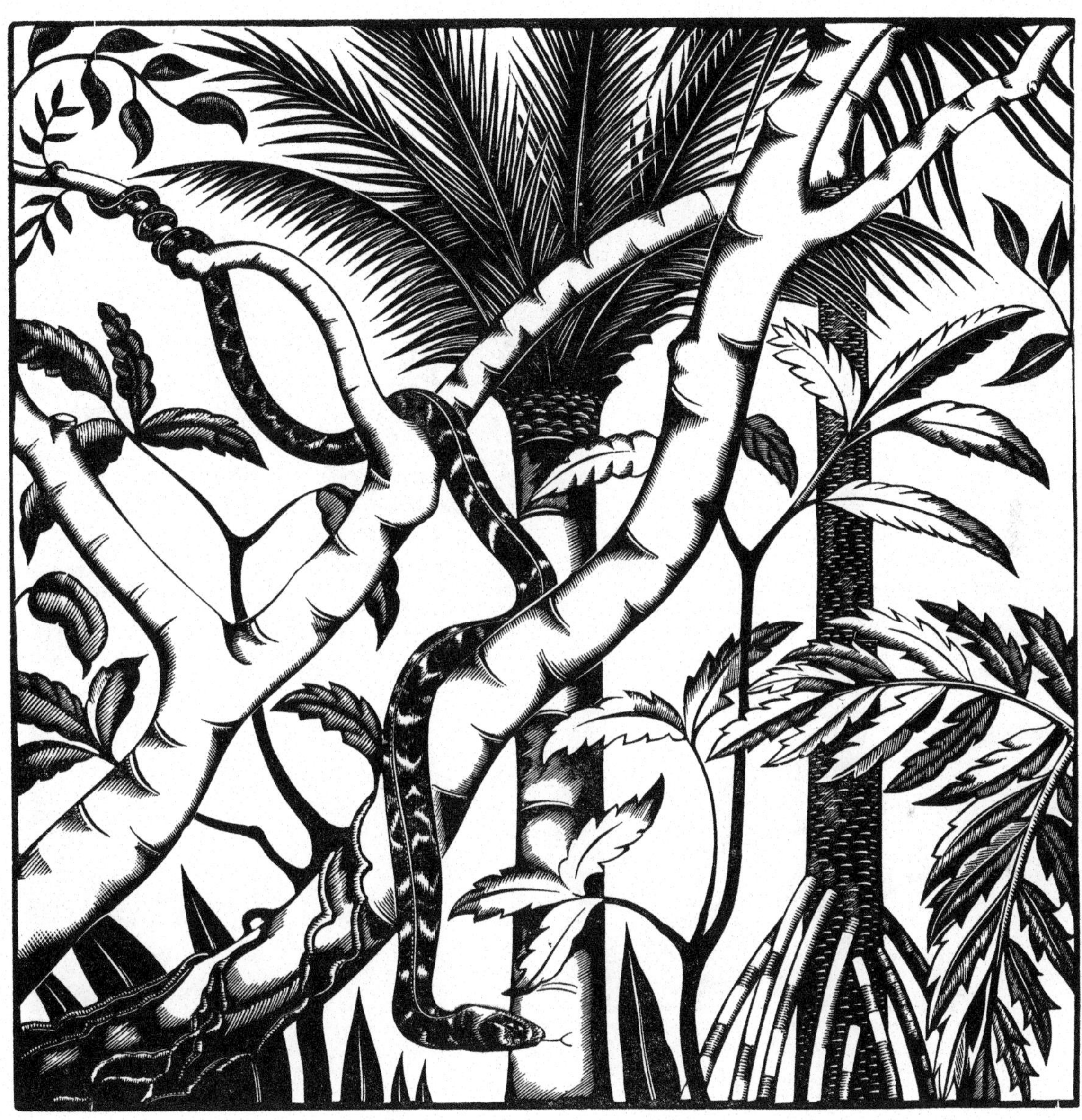

From *Glory of Life* (Golden Cockerel Press, 1934)

ROBERT GIBBINGS

← ERIC GILL. Engraving from *25 Nudes* (Dent, 1938)

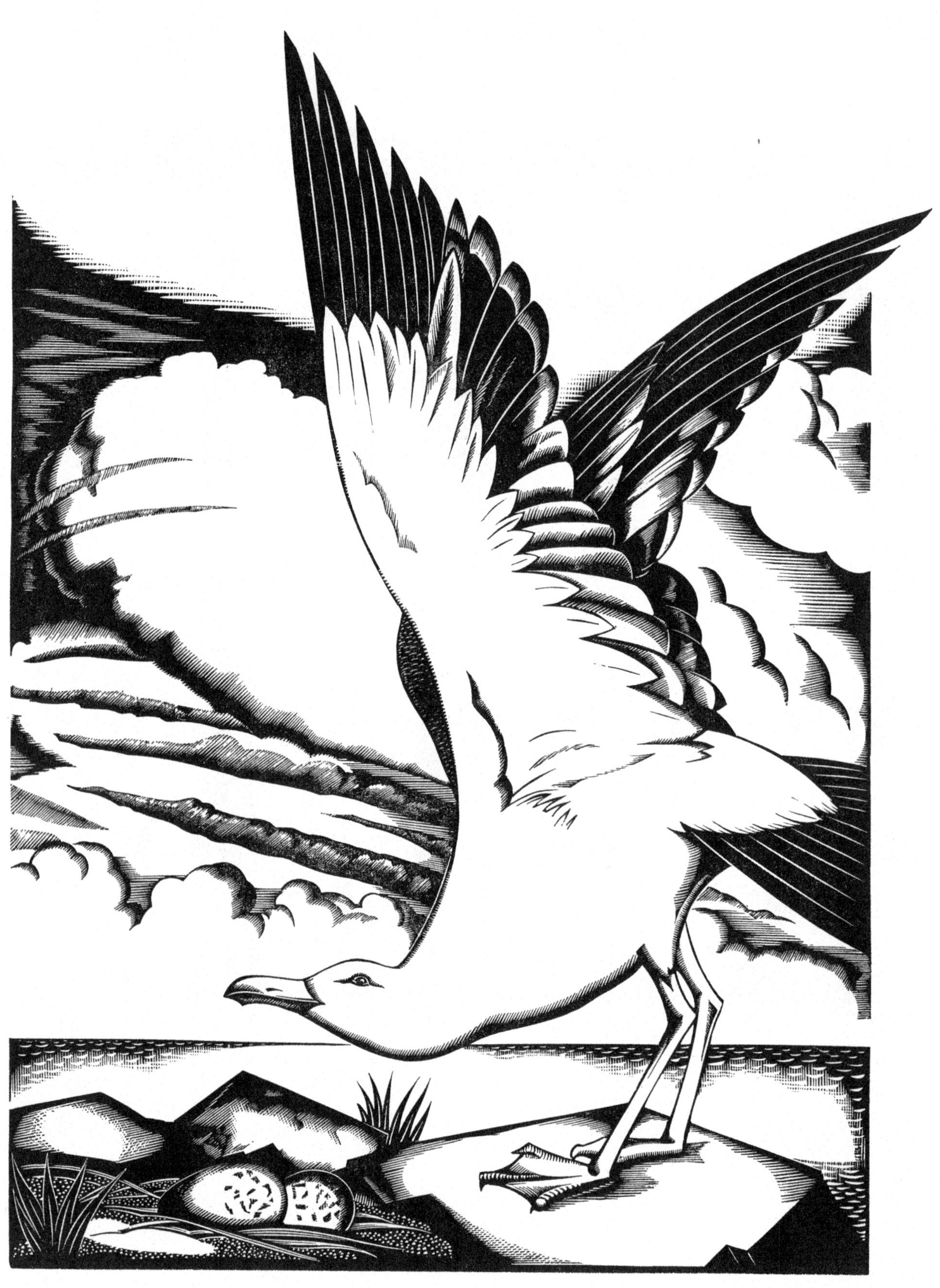

ROBERT GIBBINGS. *Glory of Life* (Golden Cockerel Press, 1934)

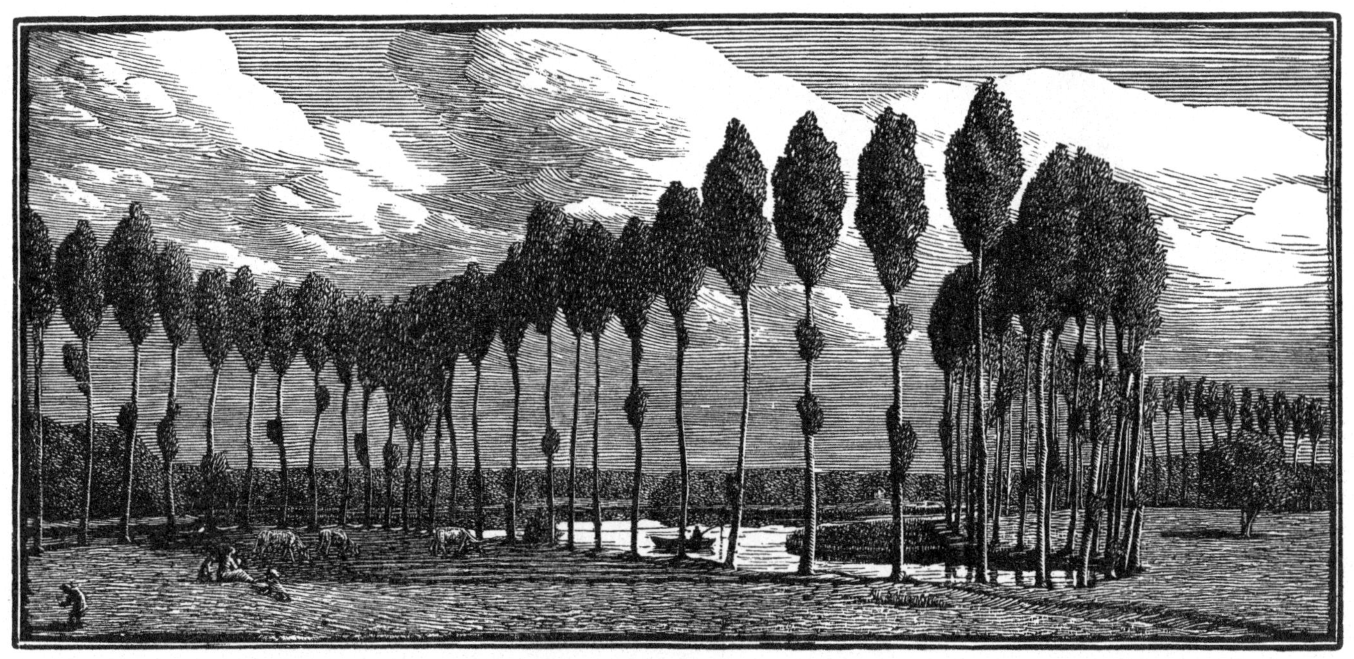

GWENDOLEN RAVERAT. Poplars, 1916

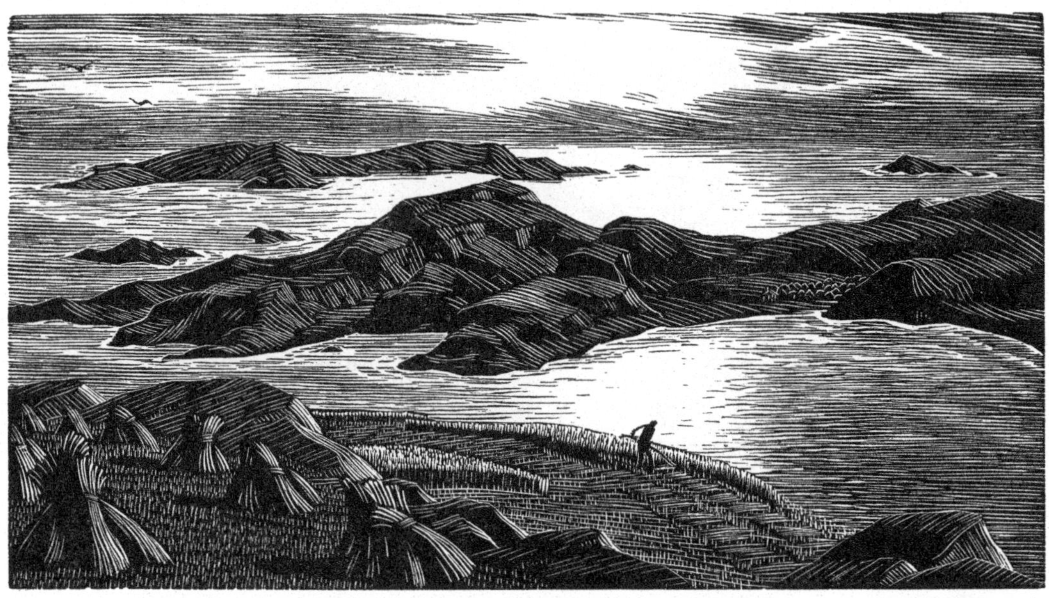

GWENDOLEN RAVERAT. Harvest by the Sea, 1918

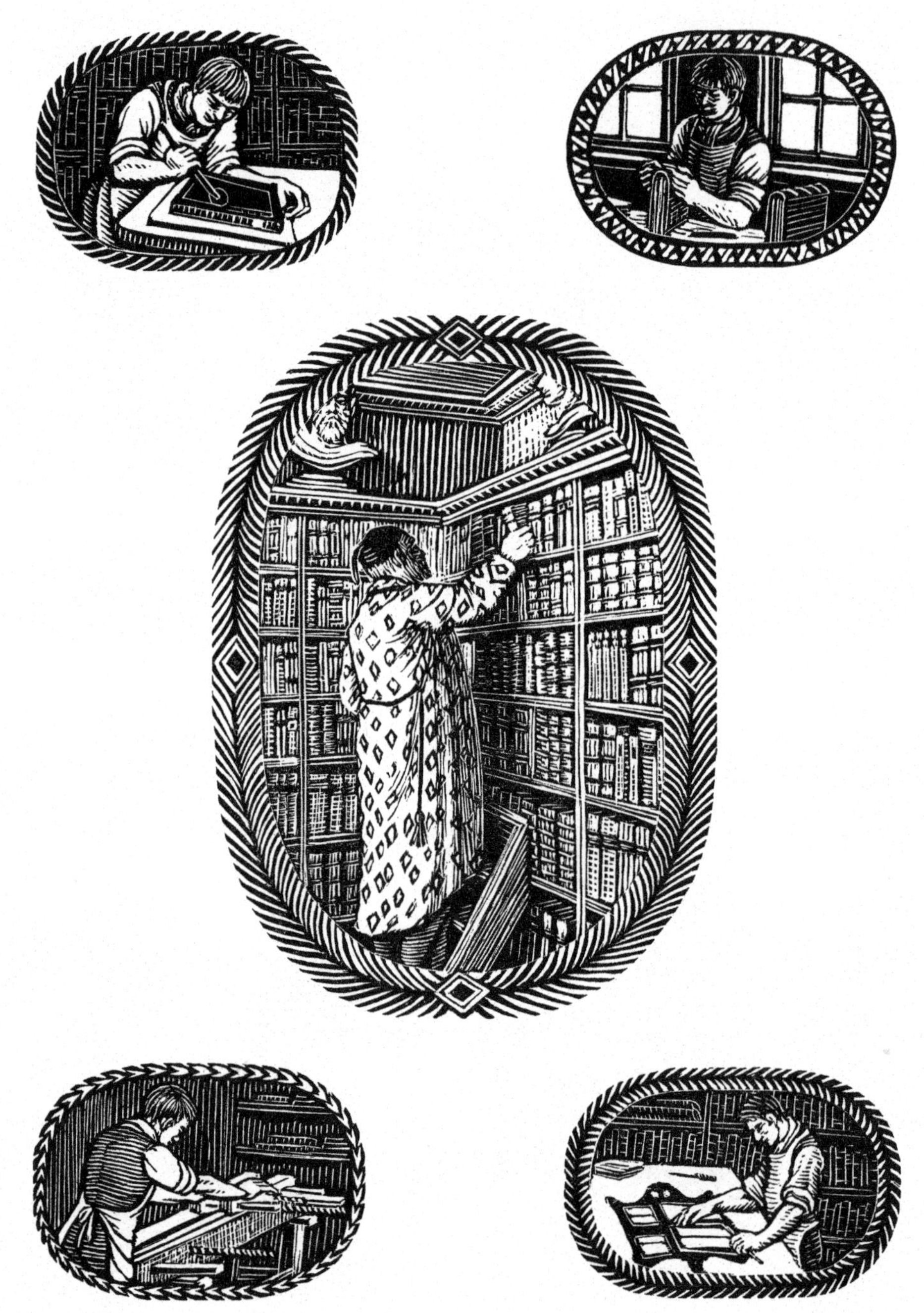

GWENDOLEN RAVERAT. Decorations for *The London Bookbinders* (Dropmore Press, 1950)

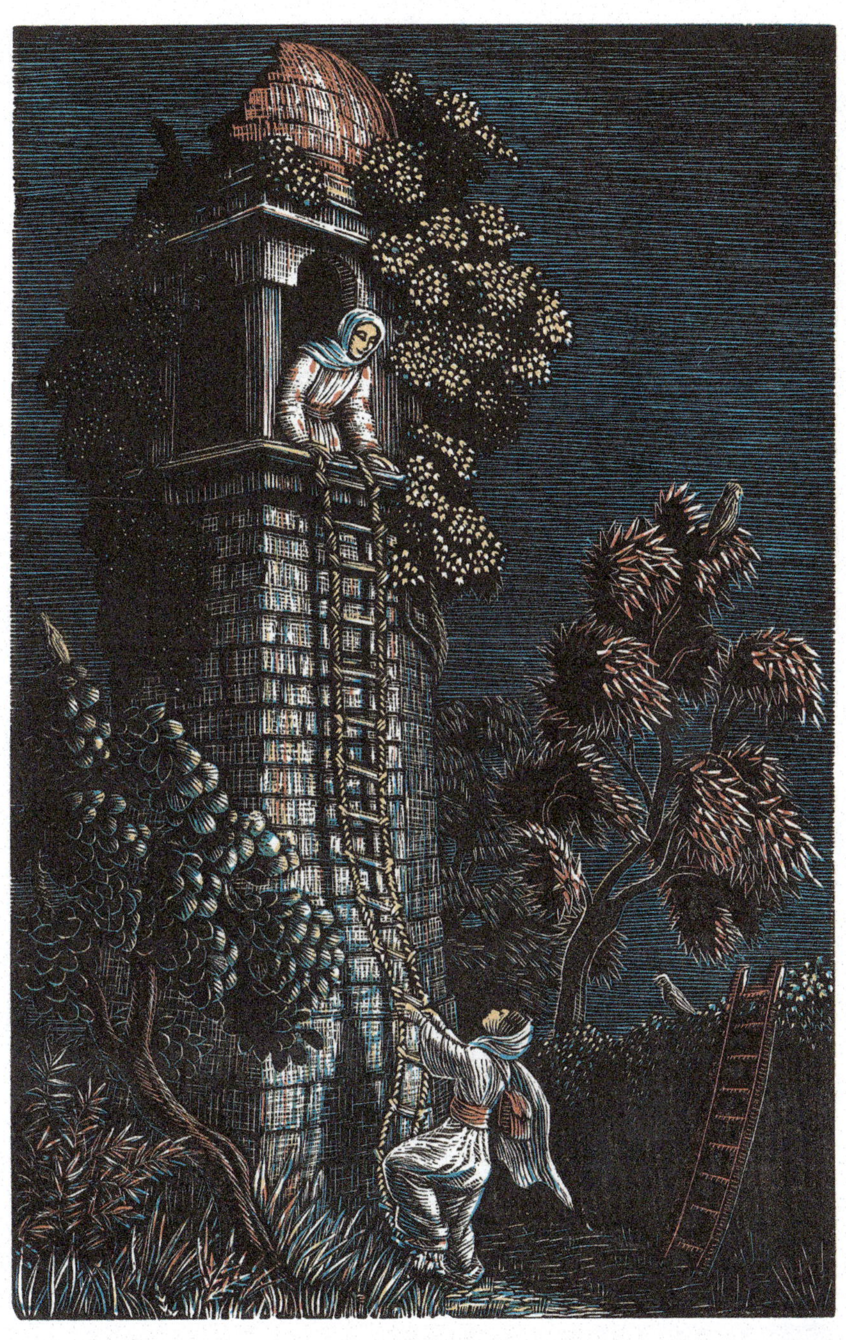

GWENDOLEN RAVERAT. The Minaret. From *The Bird Talisman* (Faber, 1939)

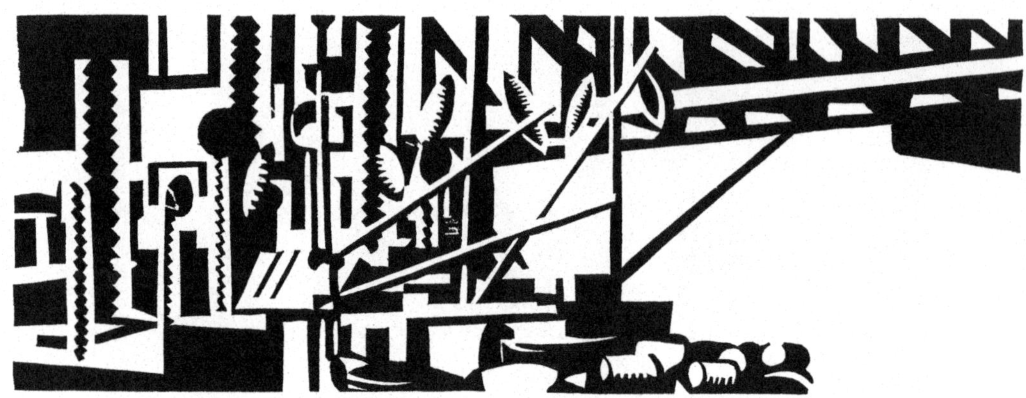

Camouflage, 1918

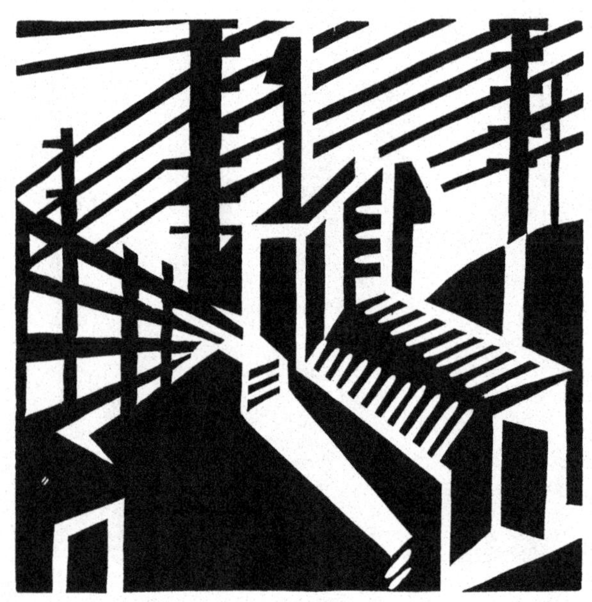

Platelayers' Sheds, 1914

OPPOSITE PAGE: In Drydock, 1918 →

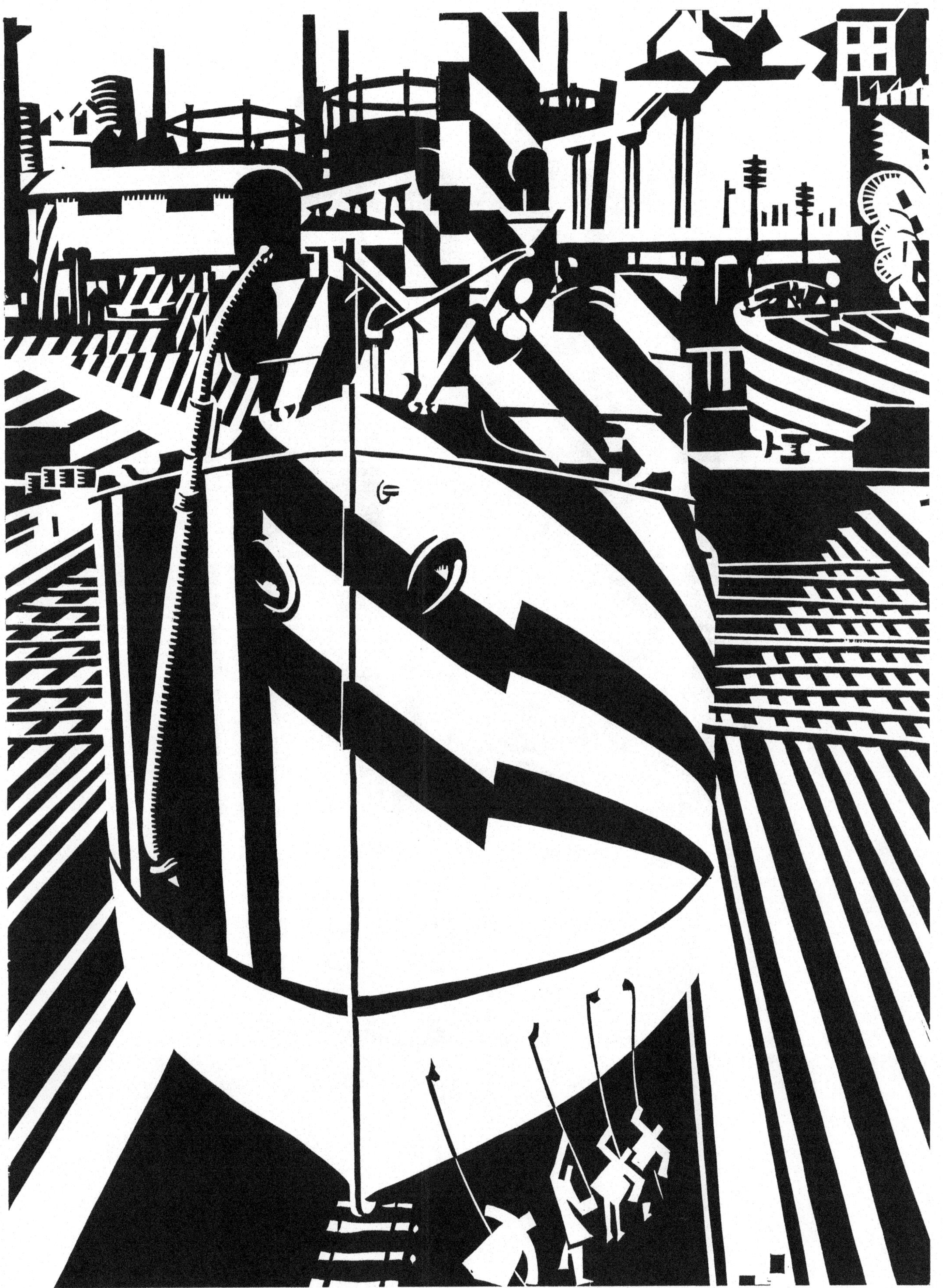

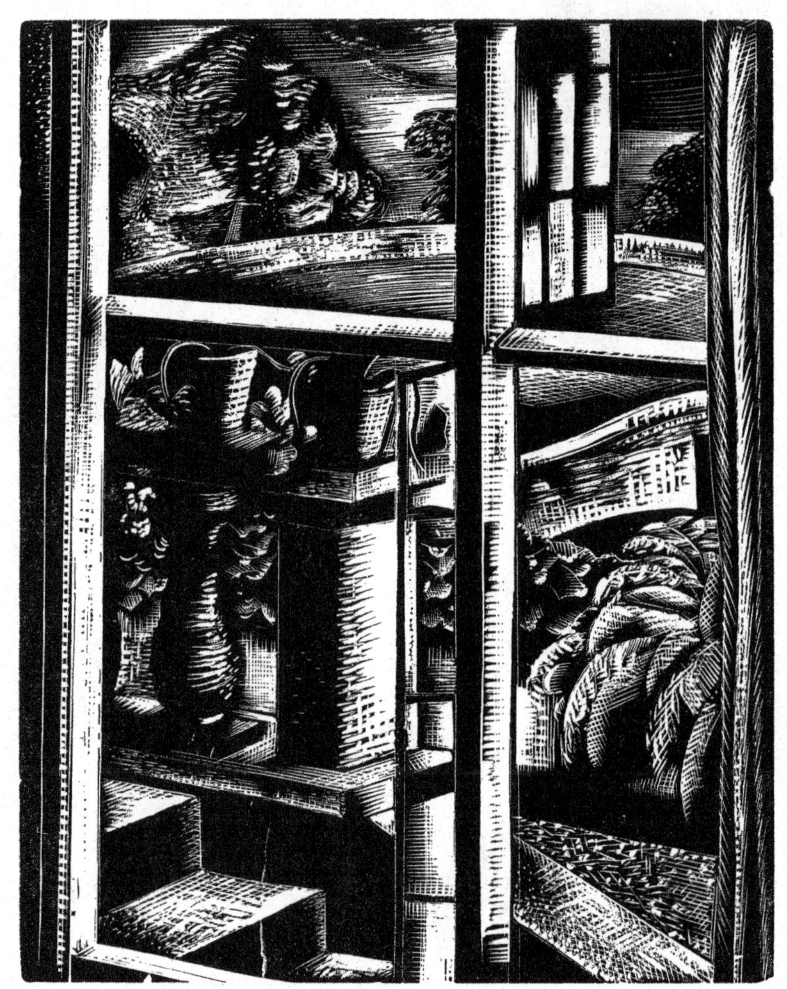

PAUL NASH. A Window in Hampstead, *c.* 1937

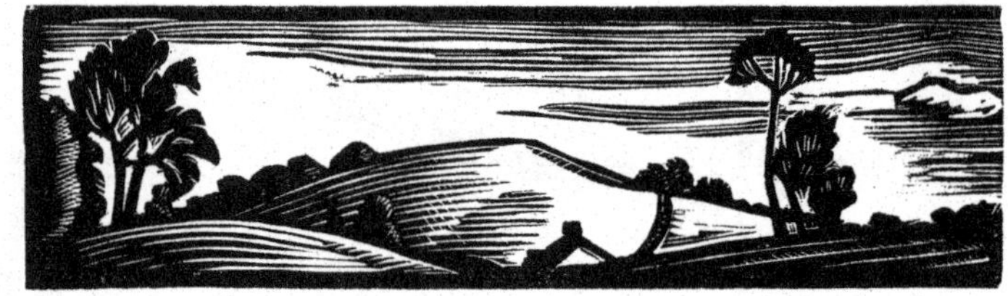

ETHELBERT WHITE. From *The Story of My Heart* (Duckworth, 1923)

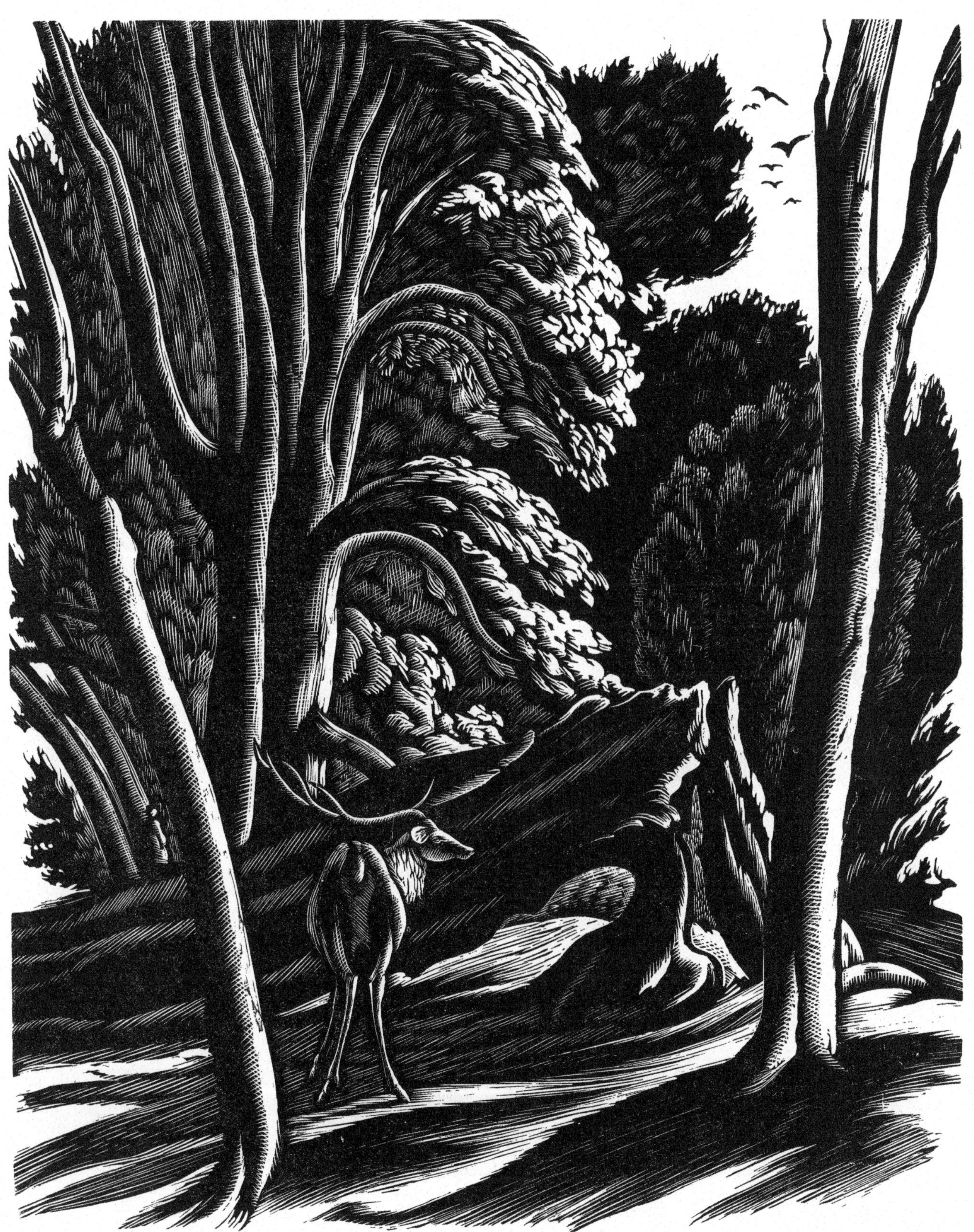

ETHELBERT WHITE. A Corner of the Forest, 1931

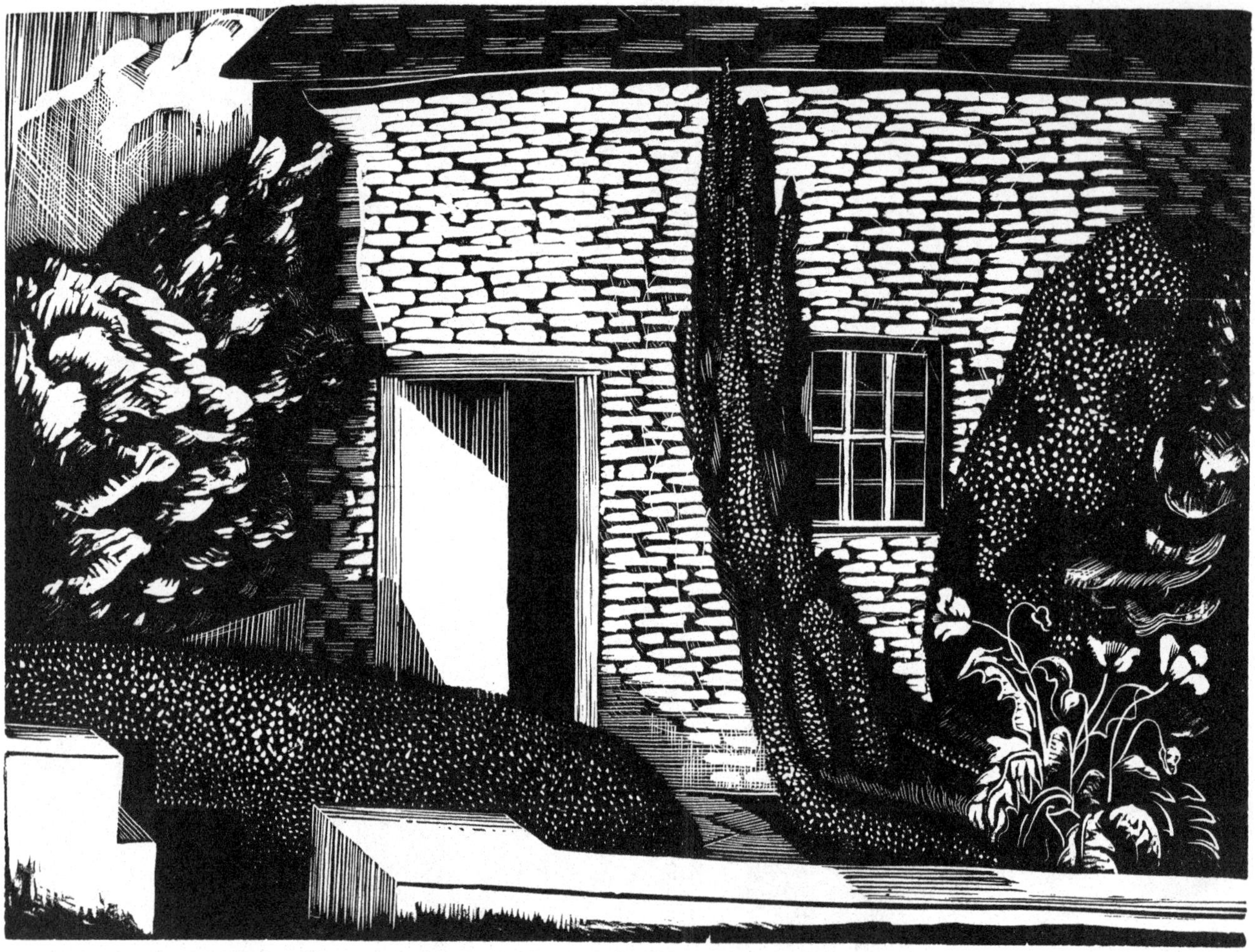

JOHN NASH. A Cottage in Gloucestershire, 1925

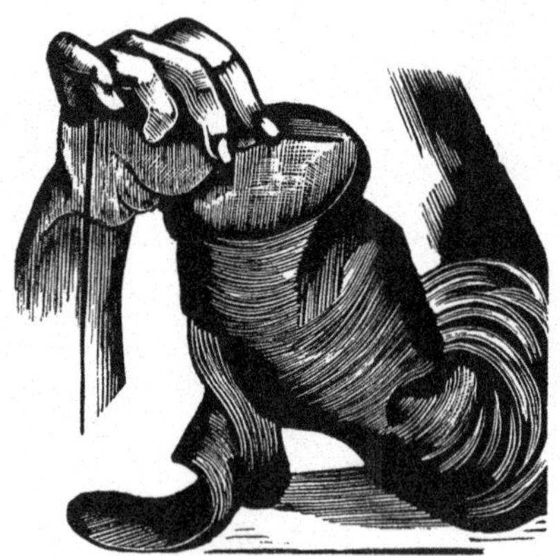

JOHN NASH. Tailpiece to *When Thou Wast Naked* (Golden Cockerel Press, 1931)

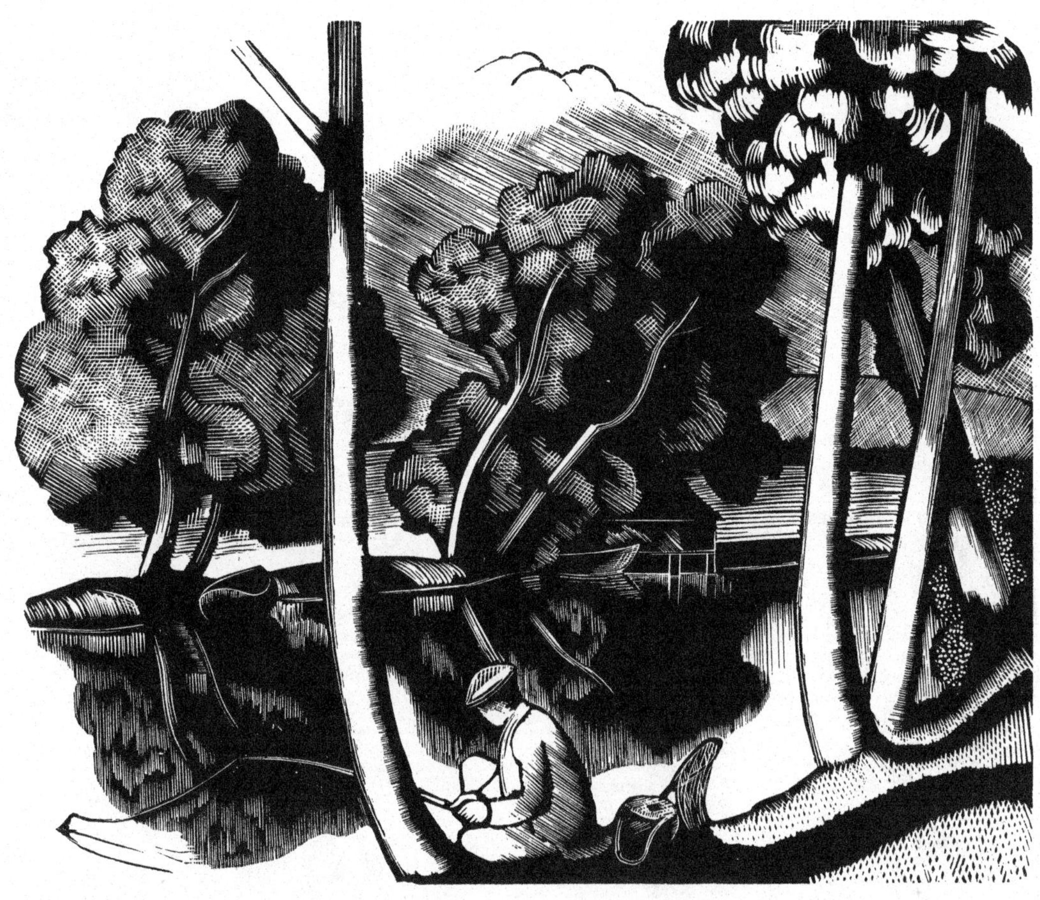

JOHN NASH. The Fisherman, 1931

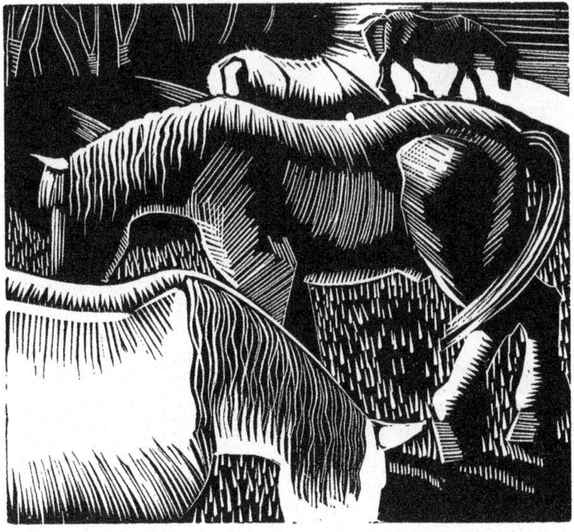

JOHN NASH. Horses Grazing, 1920

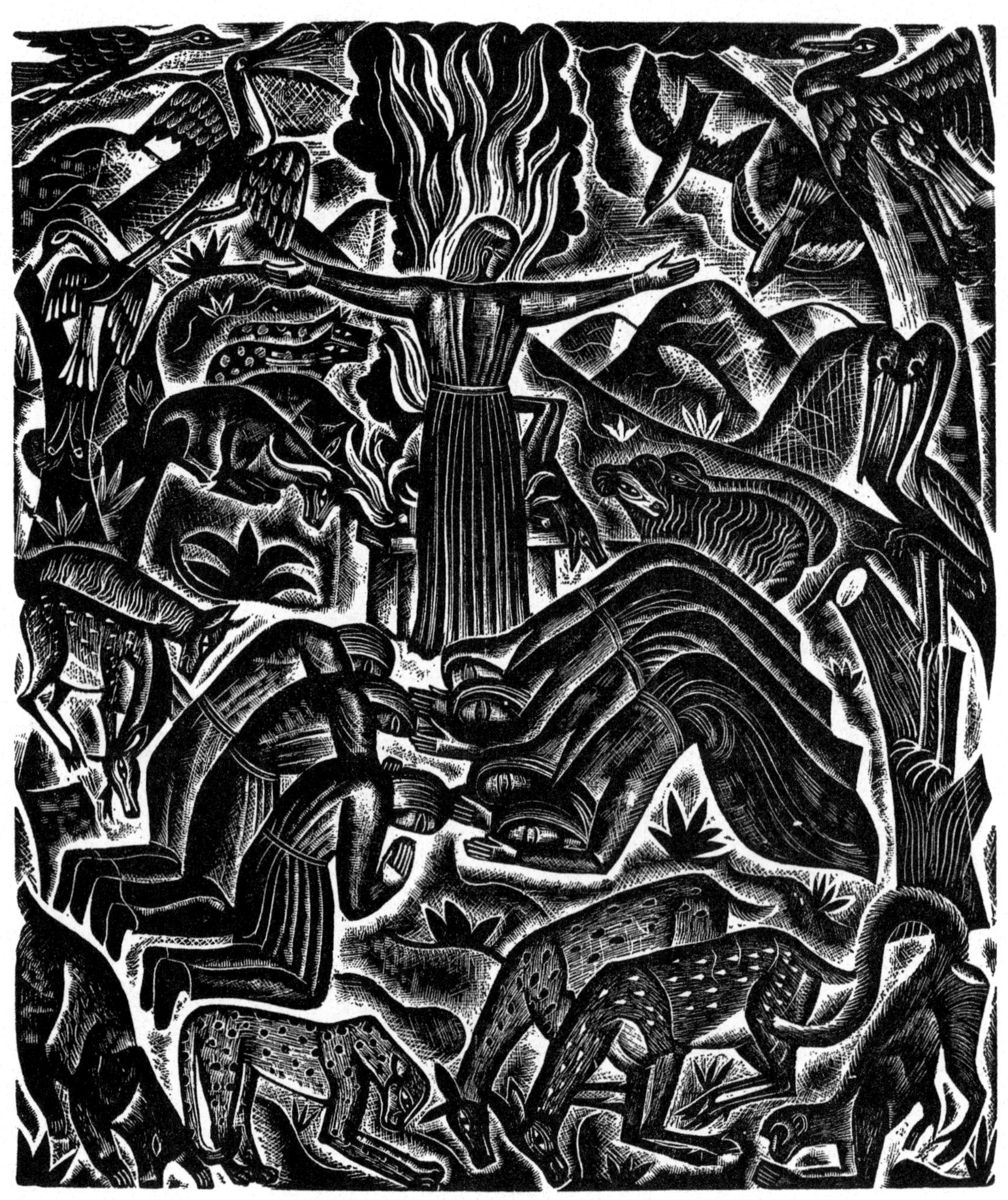

Noah. From *The Chester* ***Play of the Deluge*** (Golden Cockerel Press, 1928)

DAVID JONES

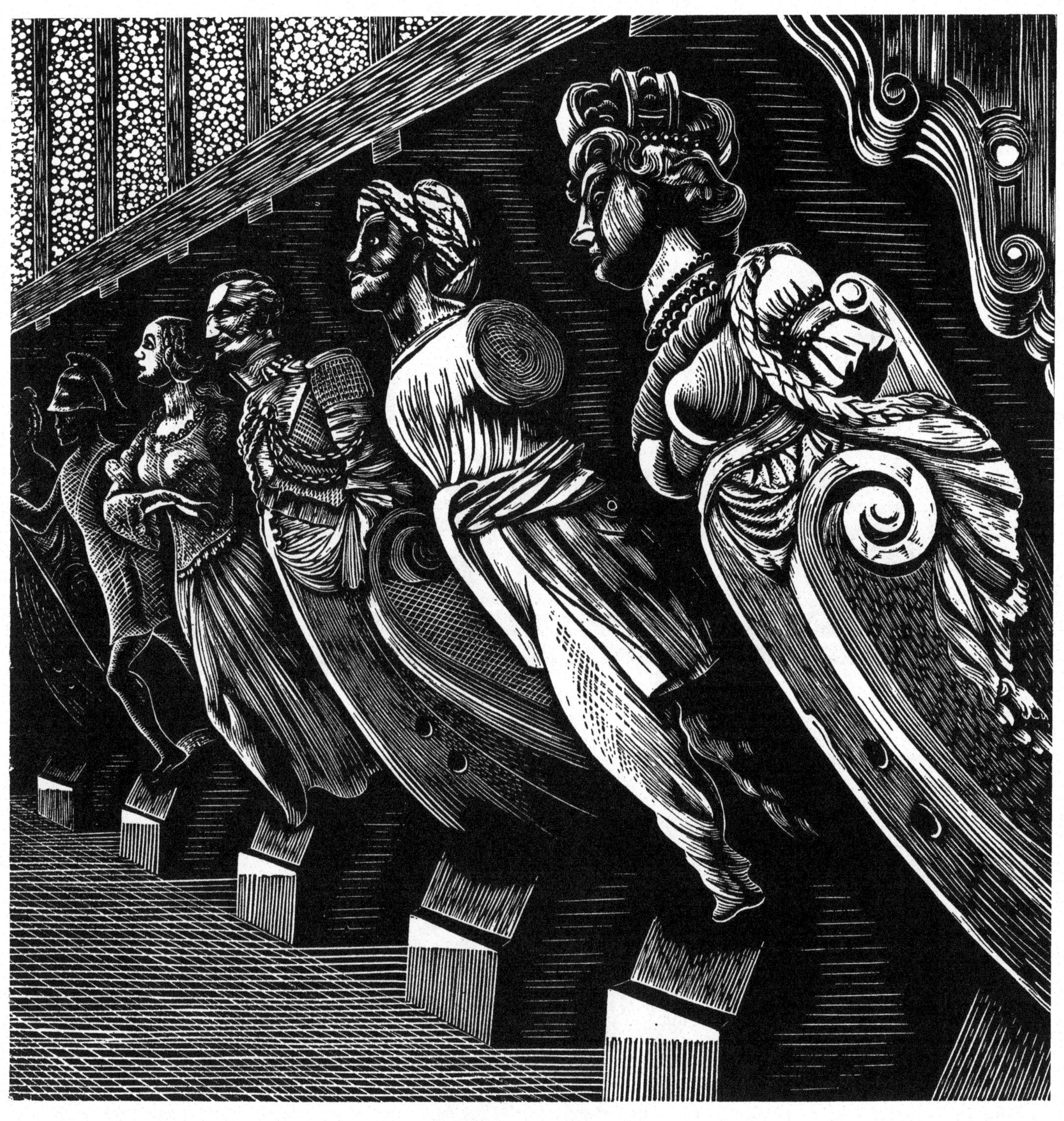

The Figure Heads, 1929

DOUGLAS PERCY BLISS

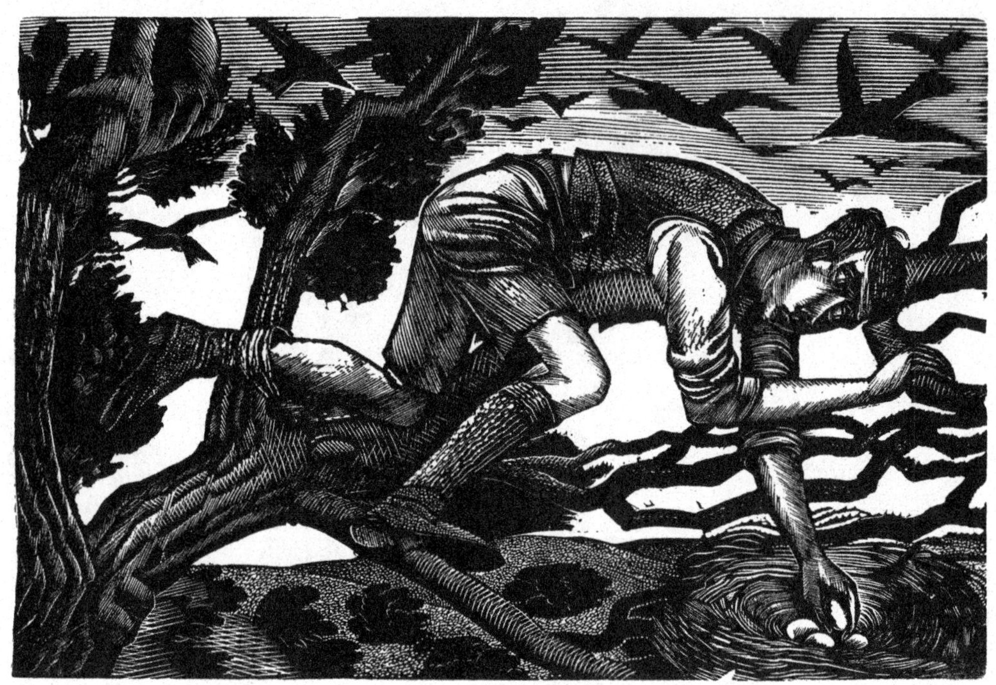

Bird-nesting, 1927

ERIC RAVILIOUS

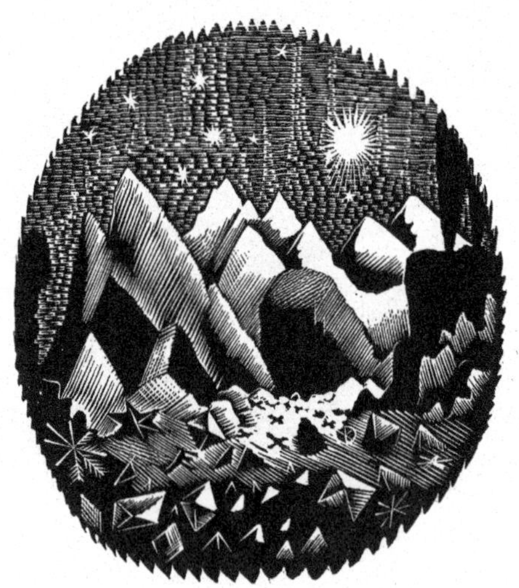

ERIC RAVILIOUS. From *Fifty-Four Conceits* (Cresset Press, 1933)

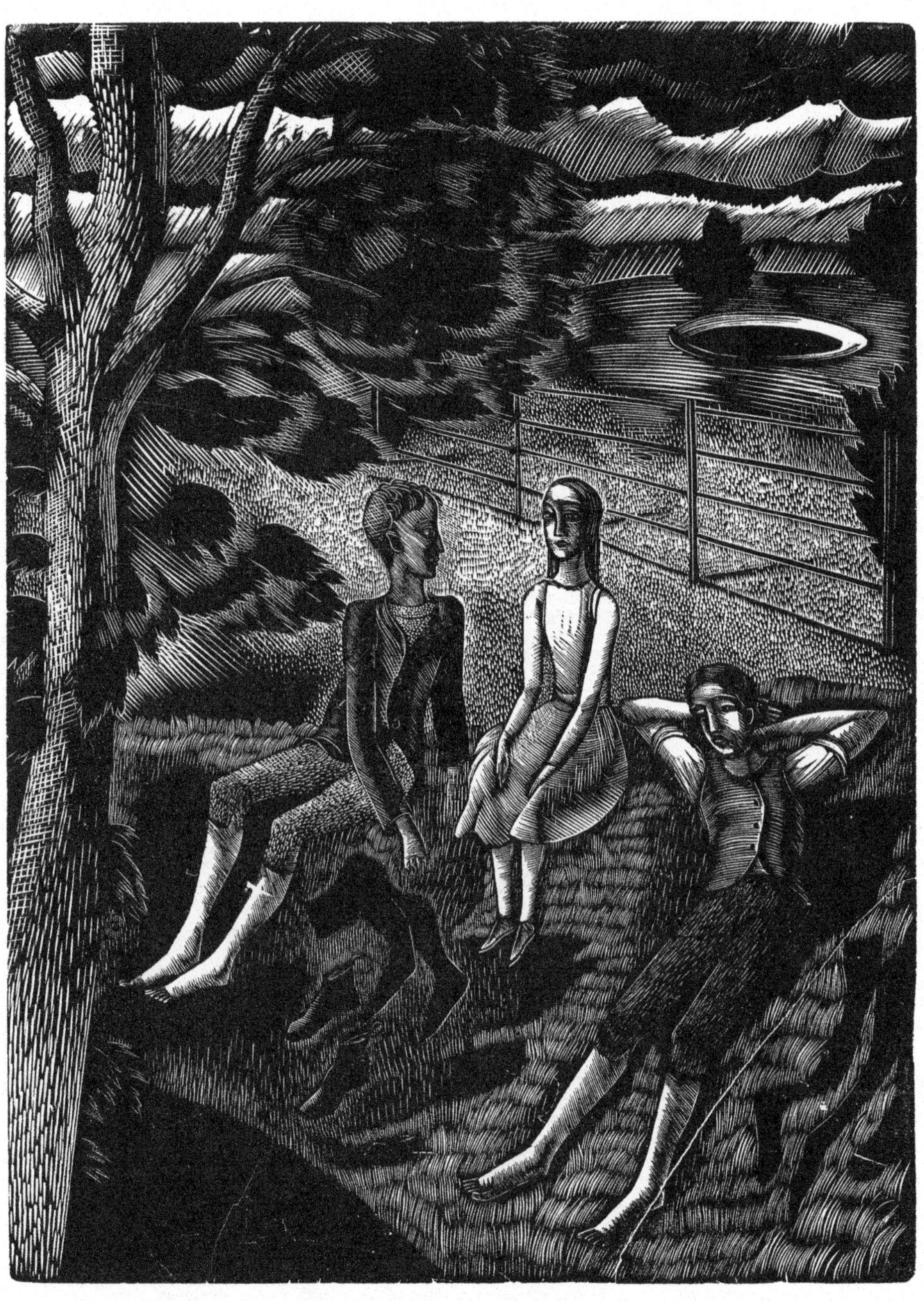

The Dew Pond, 1931

ERIC RAVILIOUS

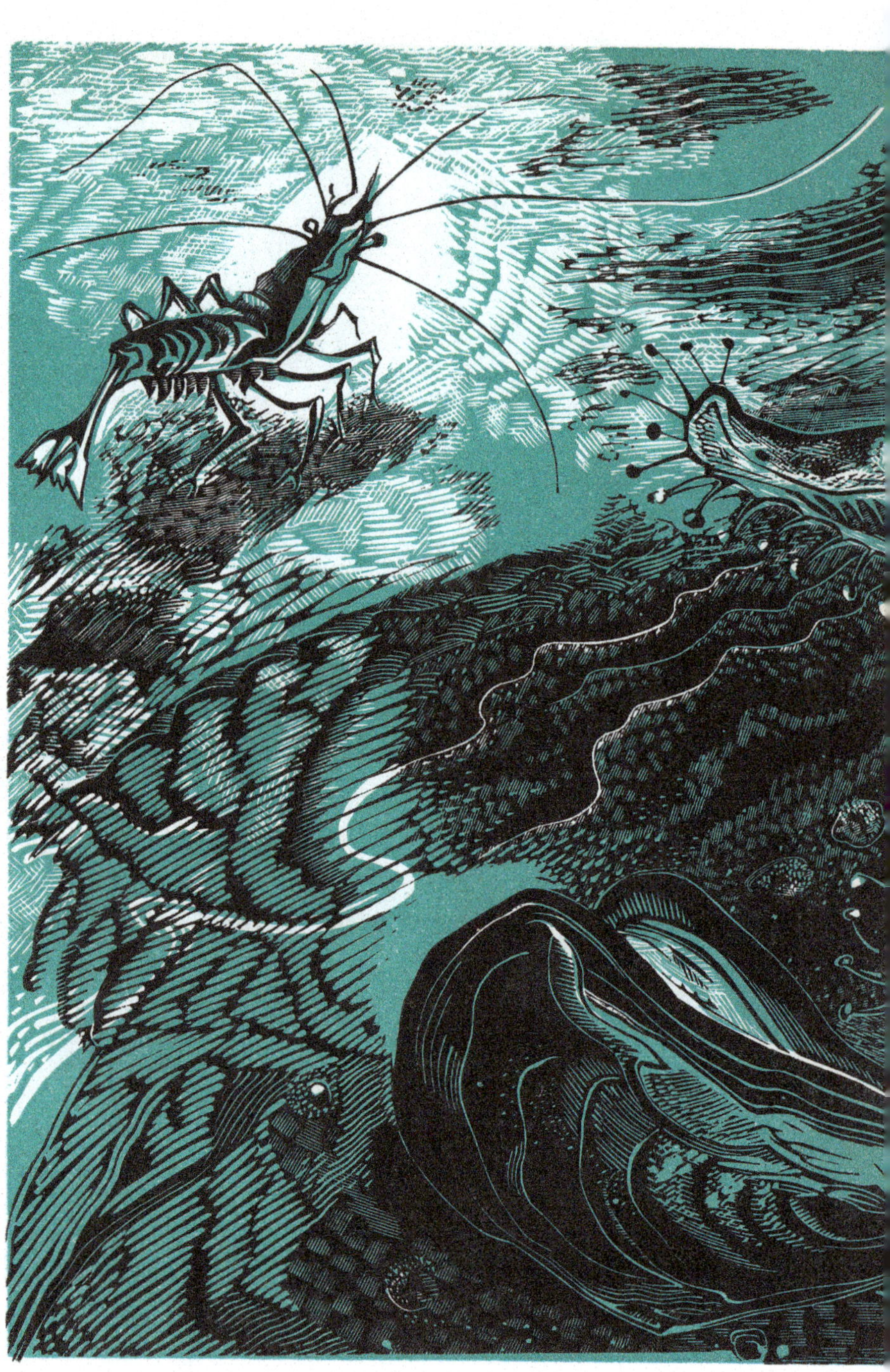

GERTRUDE HERMES

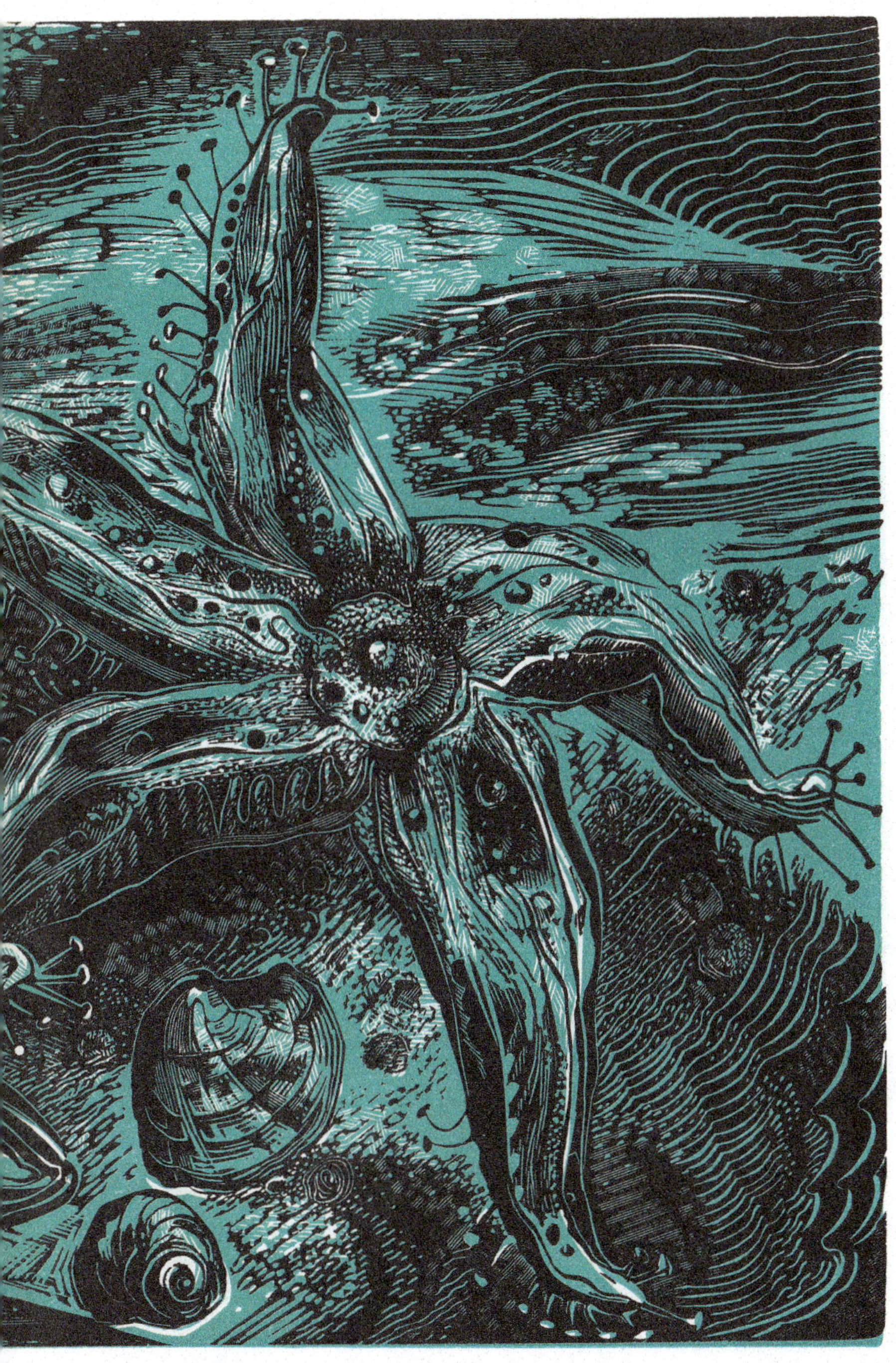

The Prawn, 1950

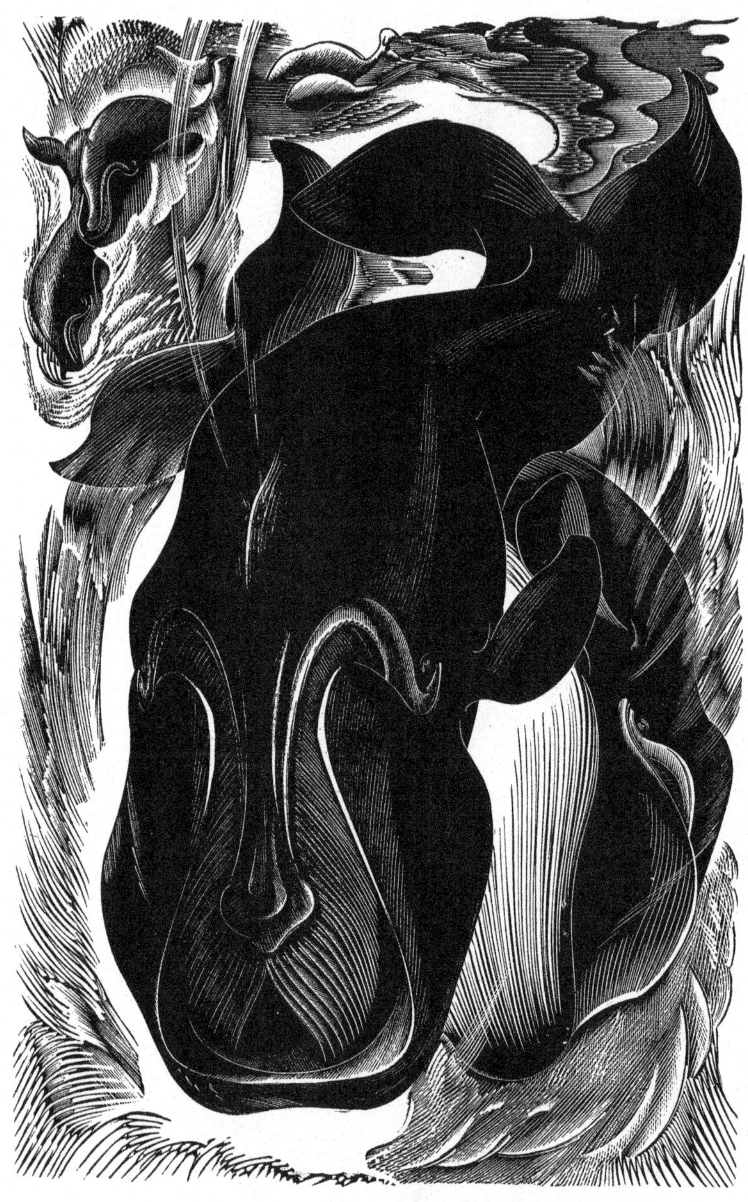

ABOVE: The Whales. From *The Ship of Death*, 1934

OPPOSITE PAGE: The Four Horsemen from Revelations of St John (Gregynog Press) →

BLAIR HUGHES-STANTON

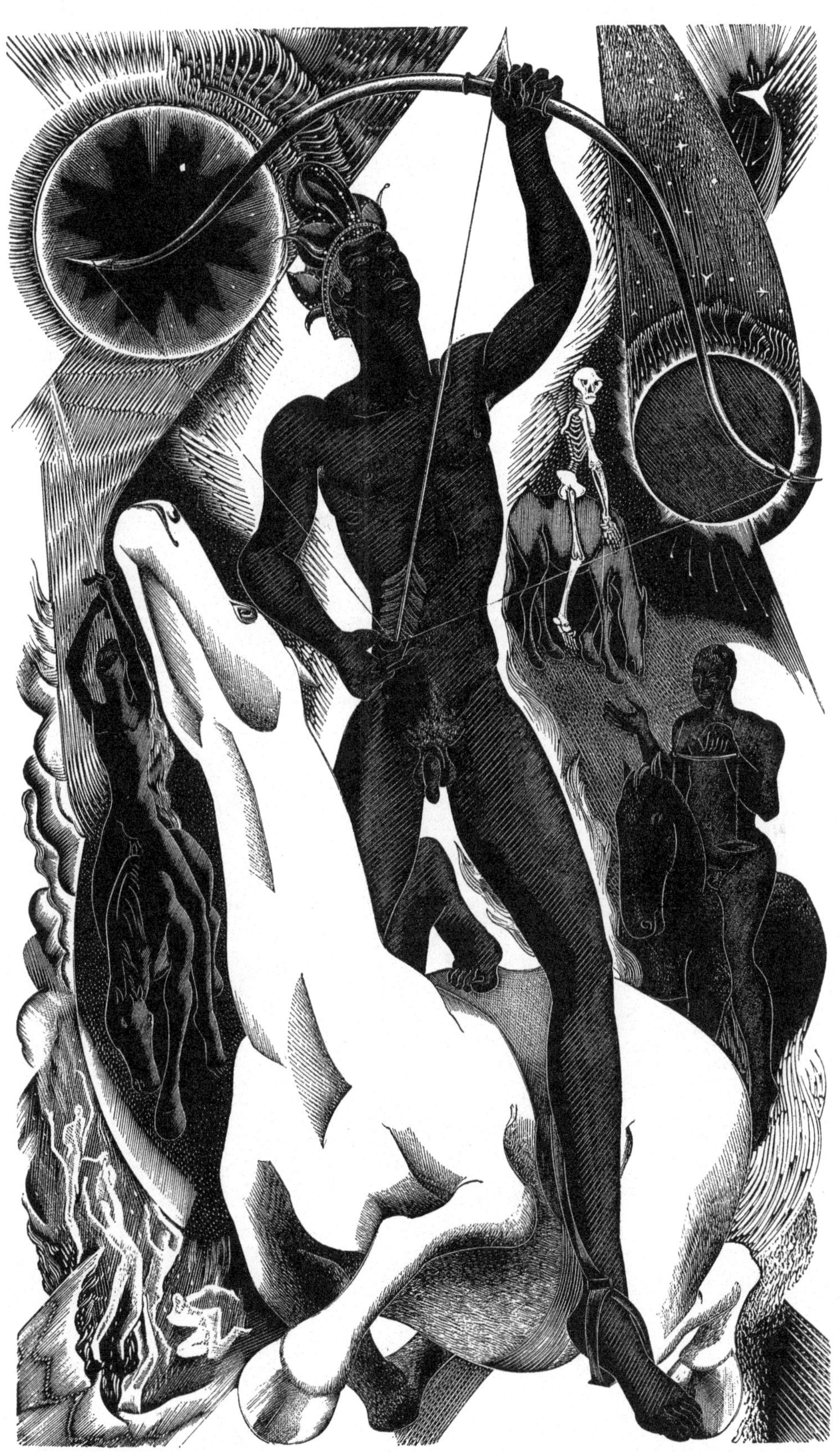

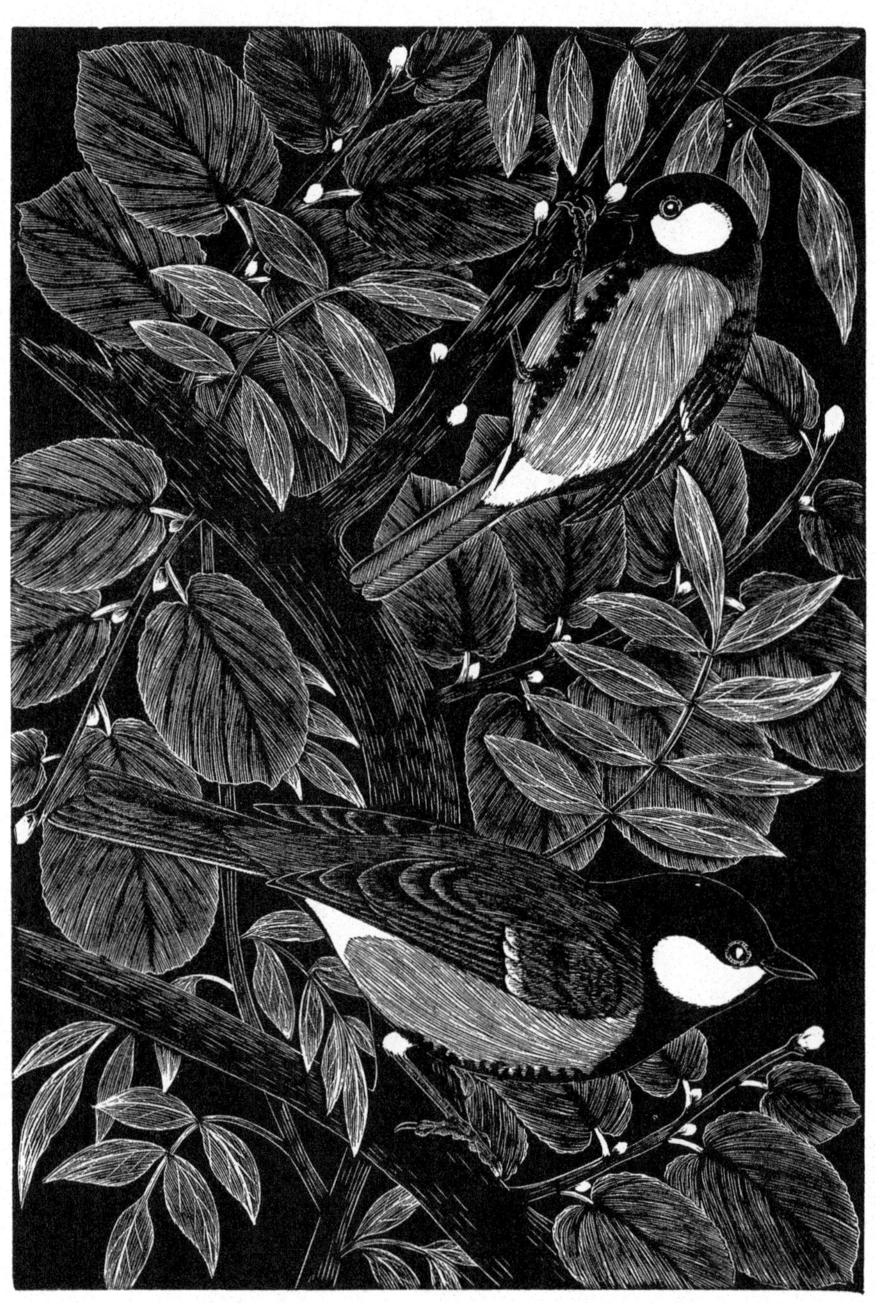

Great Tits, 1939

E. FITCH DAGLISH

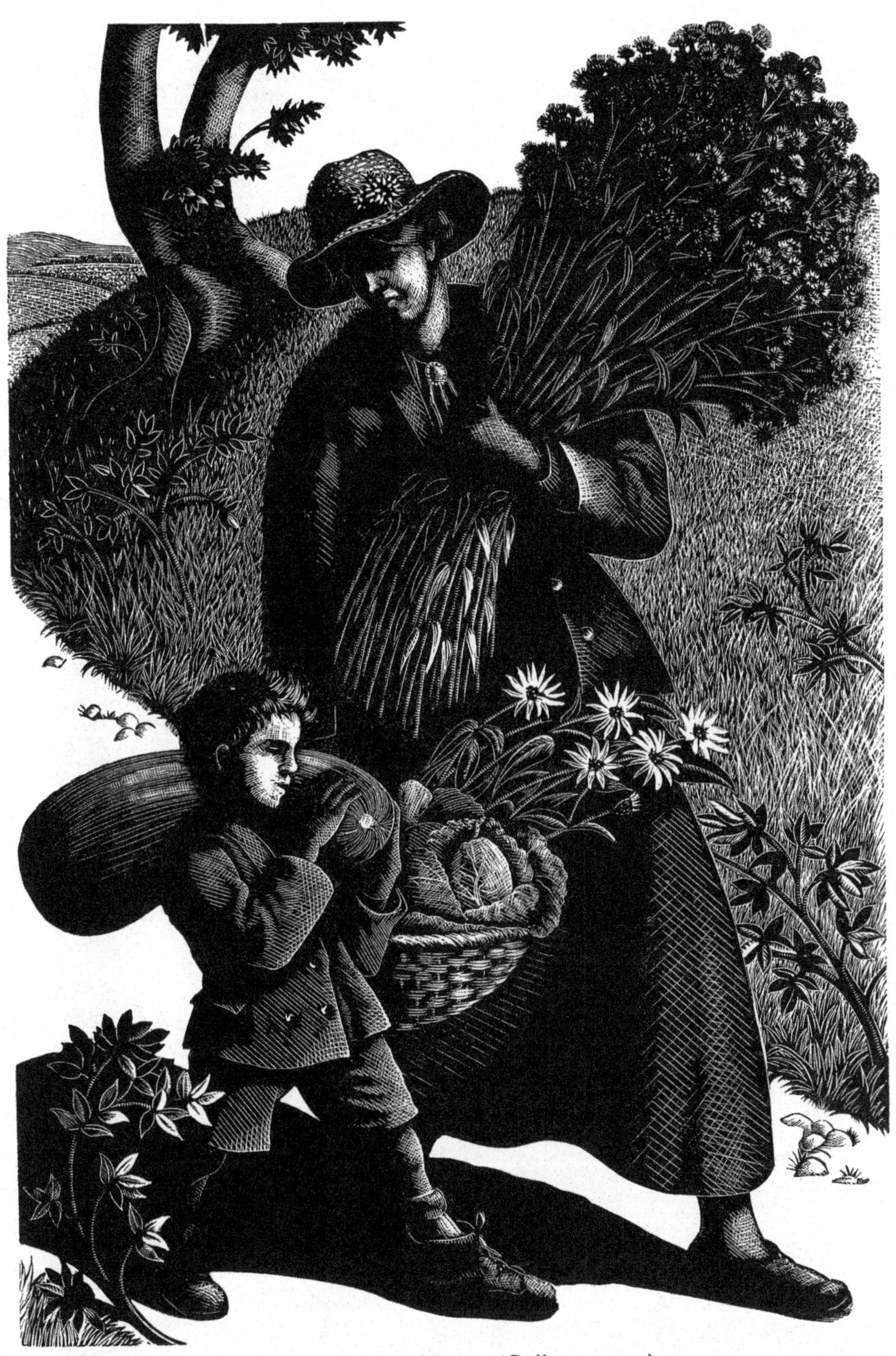

From *Country Matters* (Gollancz, 1937)

CLARE LEIGHTON

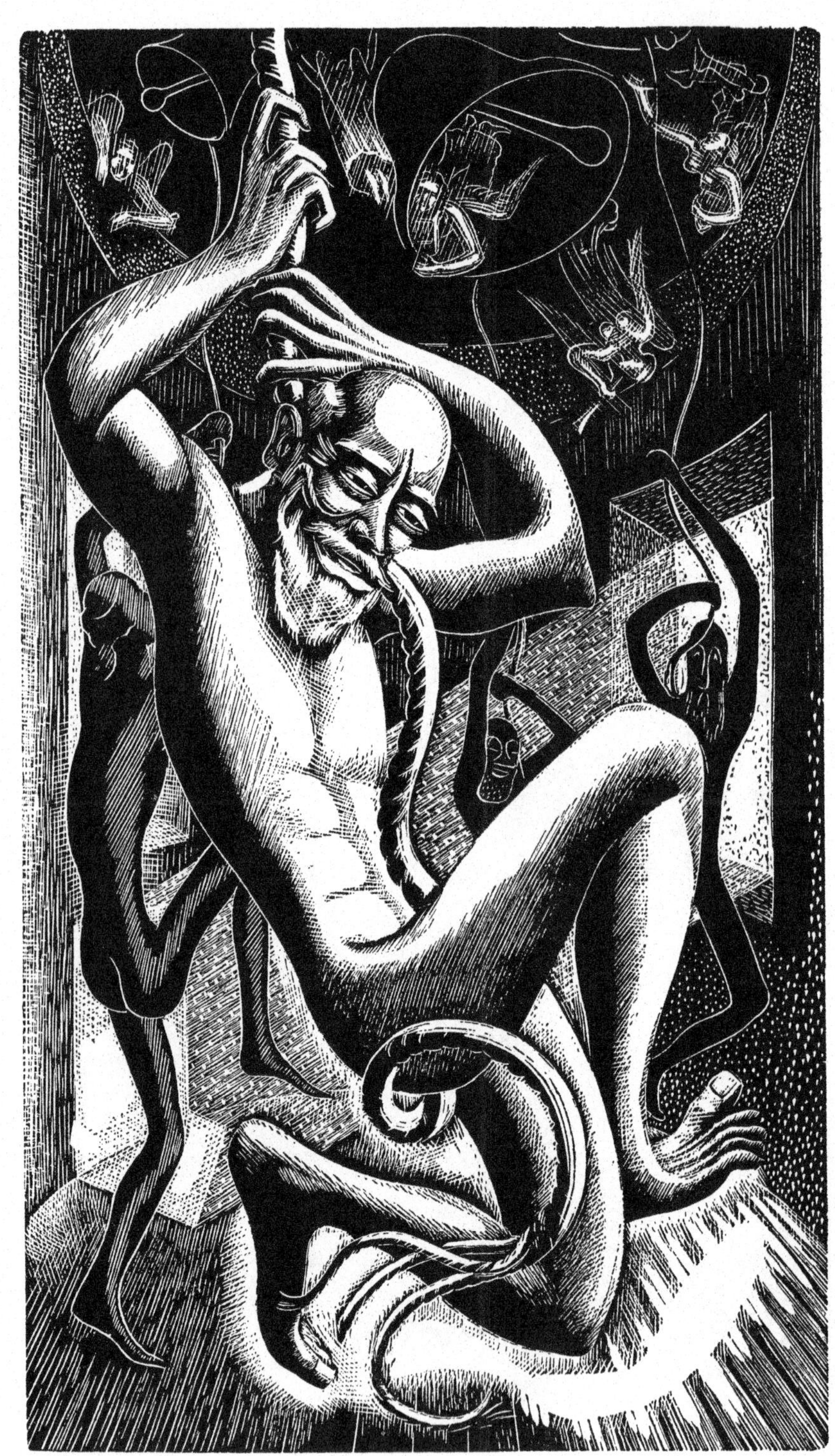

LEON UNDERWOOD. Simian Ecstasy, 1938

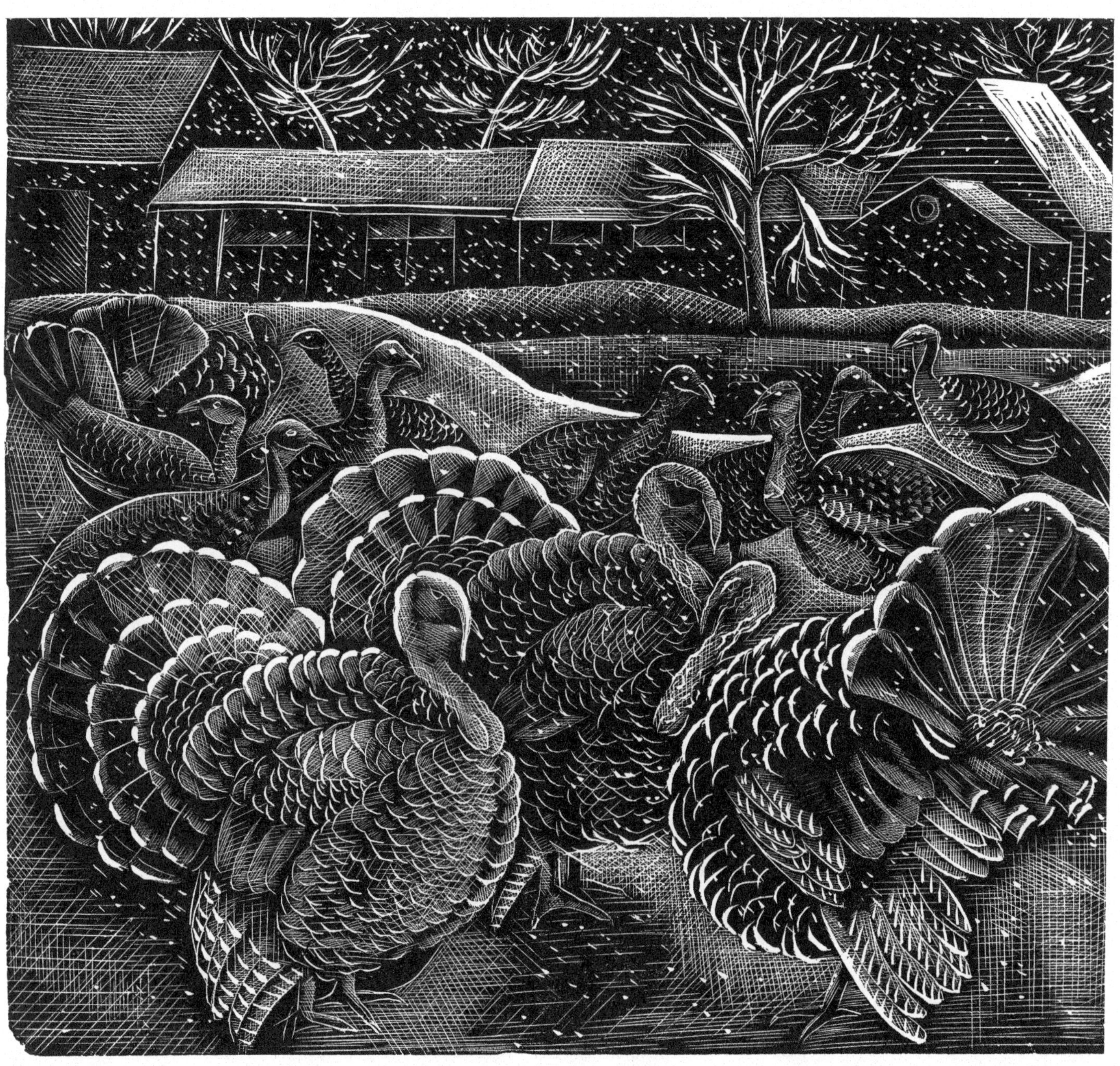

Turkeys in the Snow, 1930

MARY GROOM

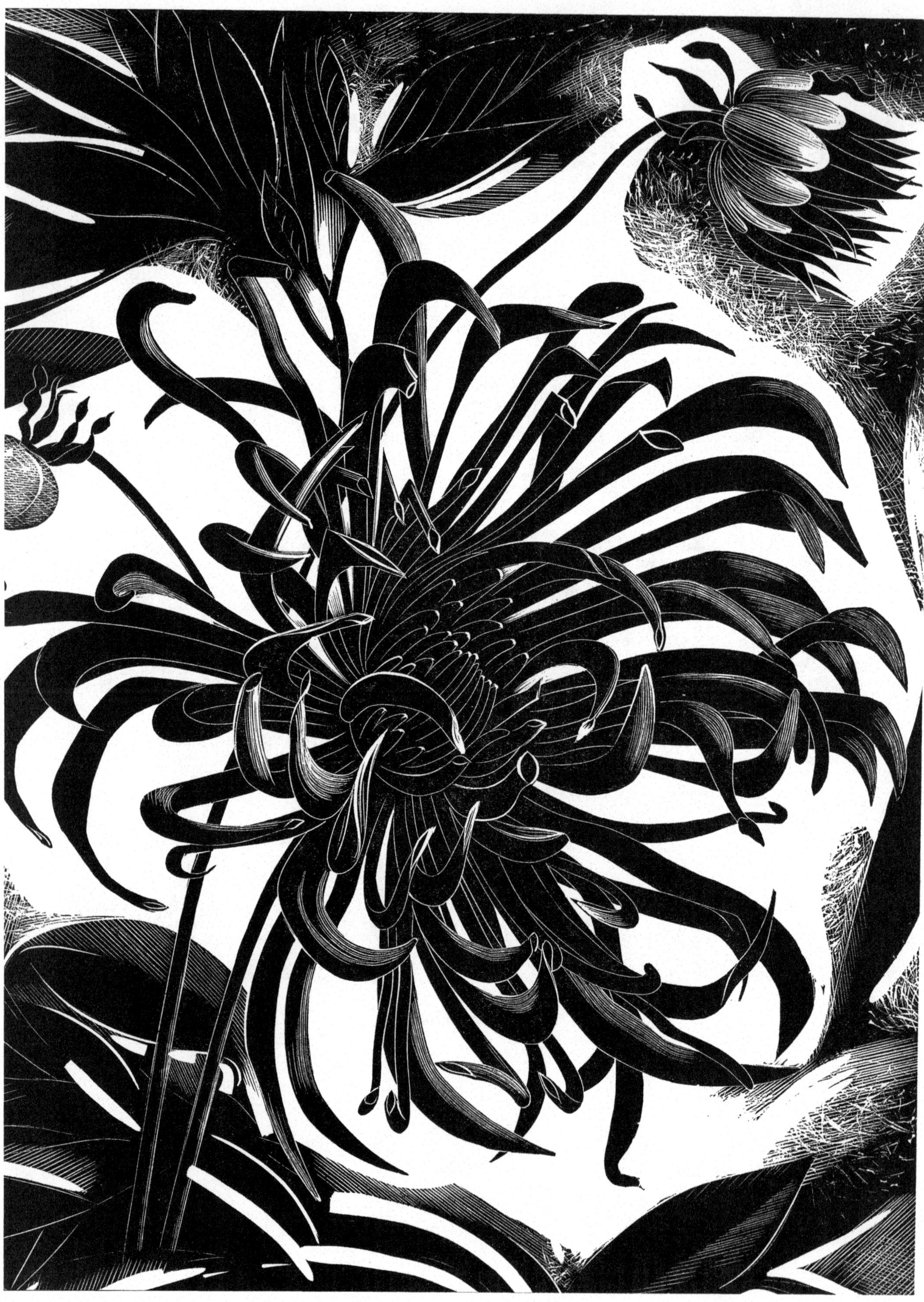

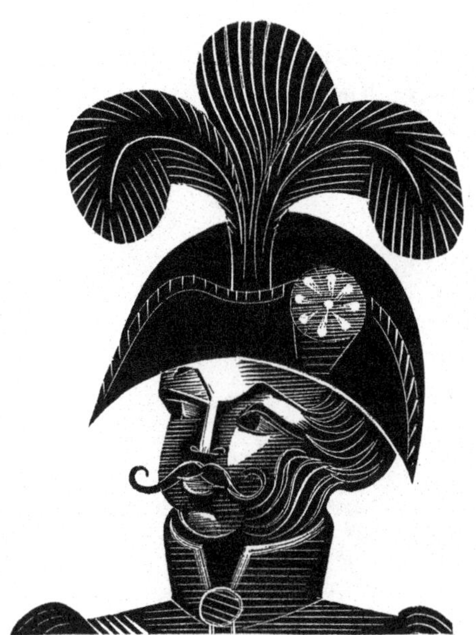

The Duke's Head

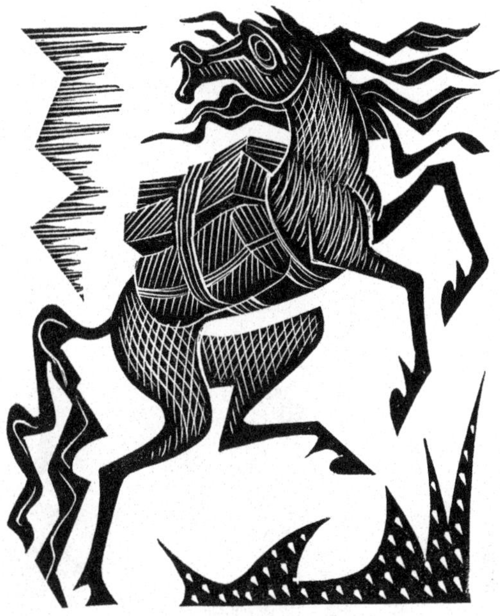

The Frighted Horse

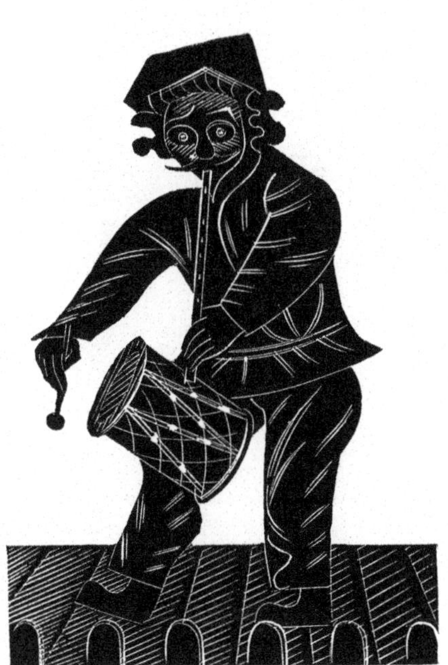

Dick Tarleton

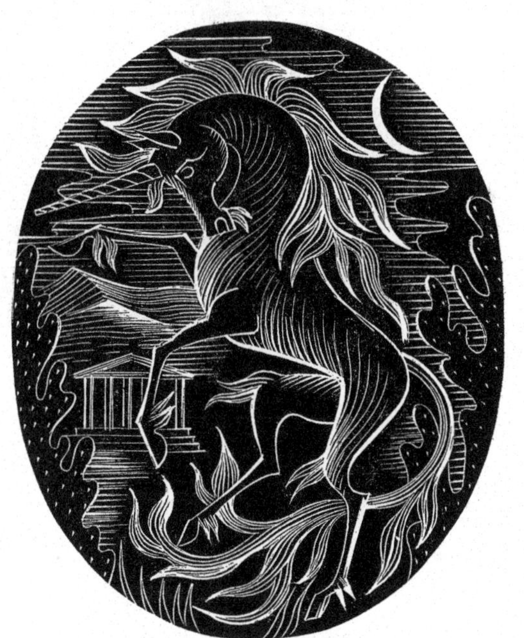

The Unicorn

JOHN FARLEIGH. Four designs engraved for the Brewers' Society, 1946

← OPPOSITE PAGE: JOHN FARLEIGH. Detail of a large flower engraving, 1950

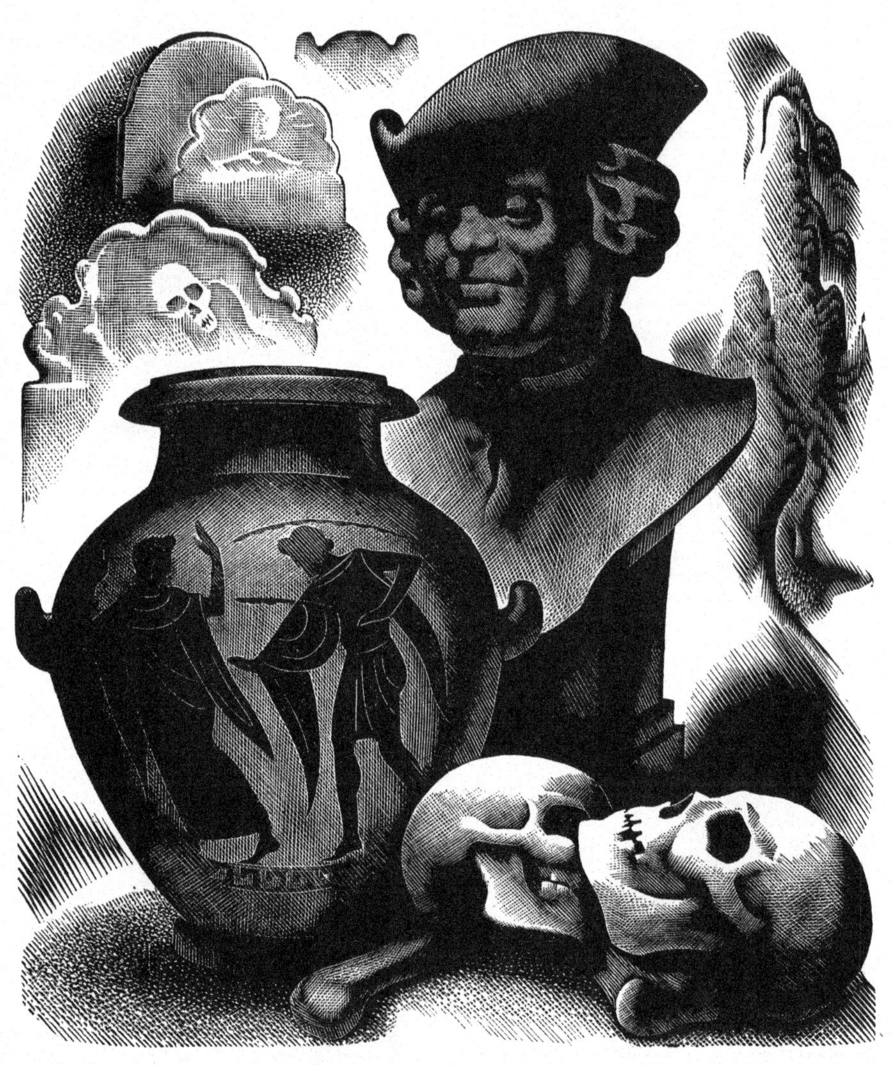

'Can Storied Urn . . .' 1938

AGNES MILLER-PARKER

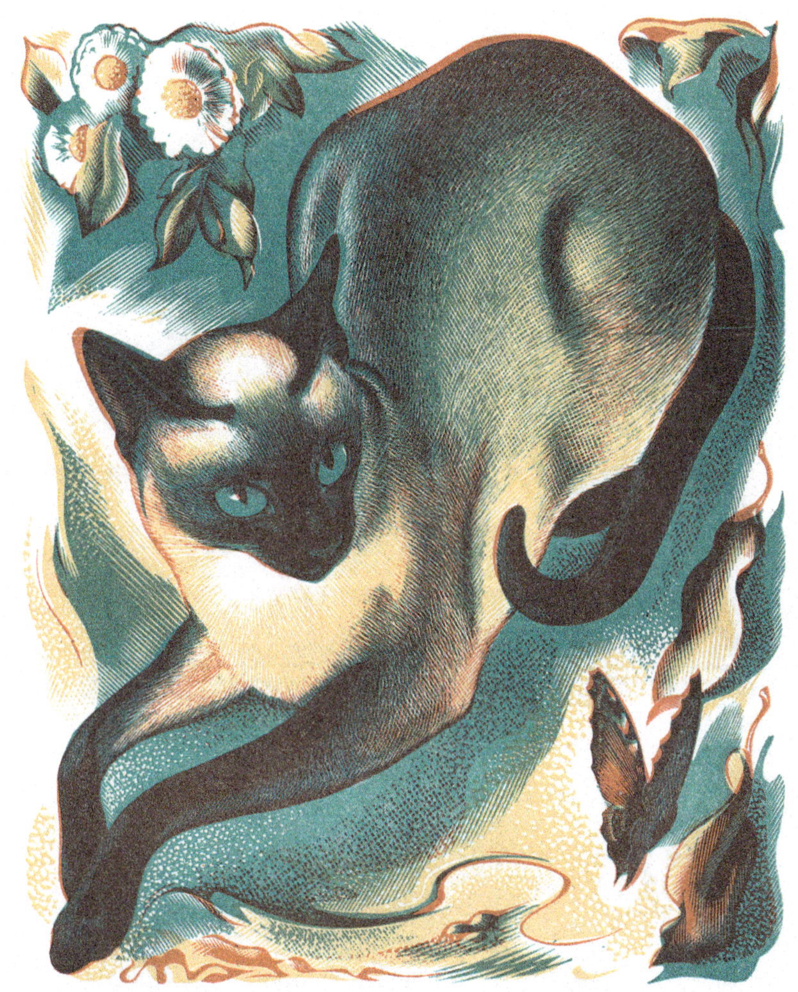

Siamese Cat, 1939

AGNES MILLER-PARKER

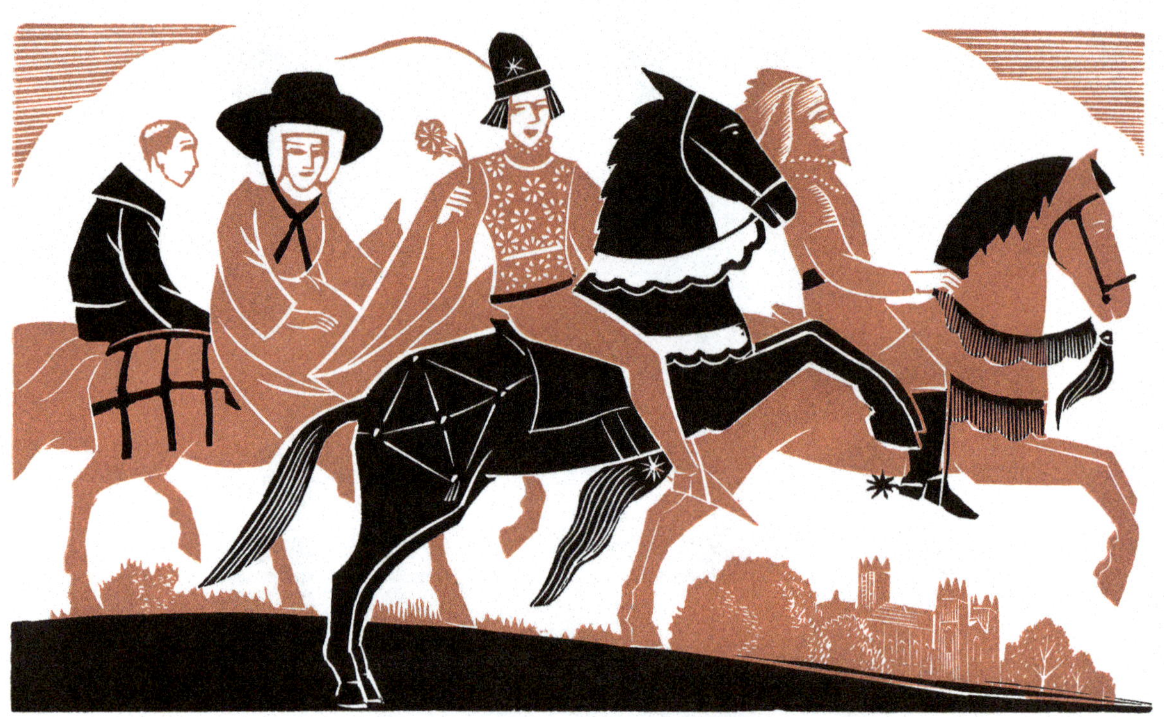

IAIN MACNAB. *Canterbury Pilgrims*, 1938

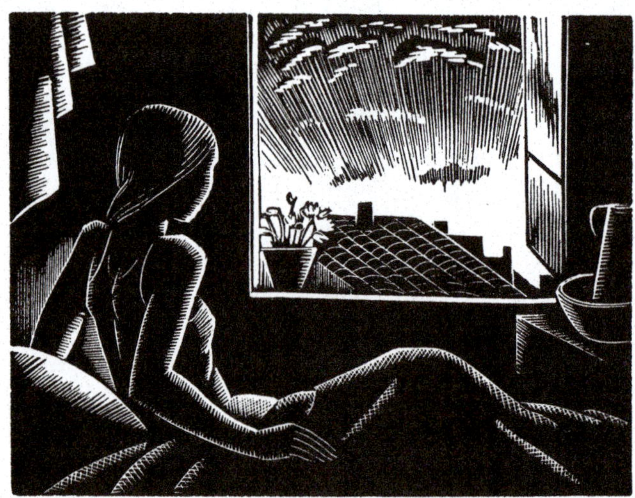

IAIN MACNAB. Morning. From *Pippa Passes* (Penguin, 1937)

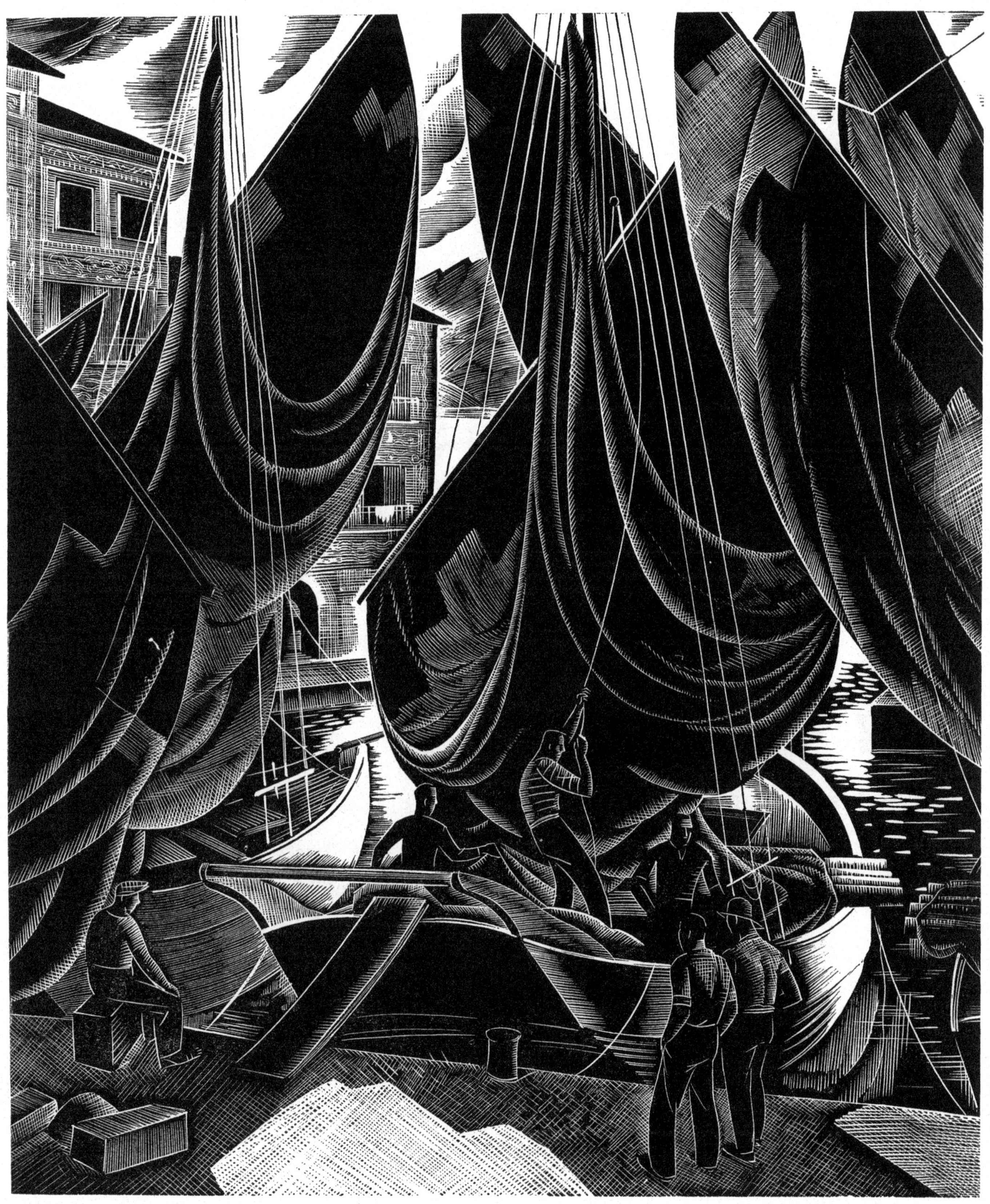

IAIN MACNAB. Drying Sails, Lake Garda, 1938

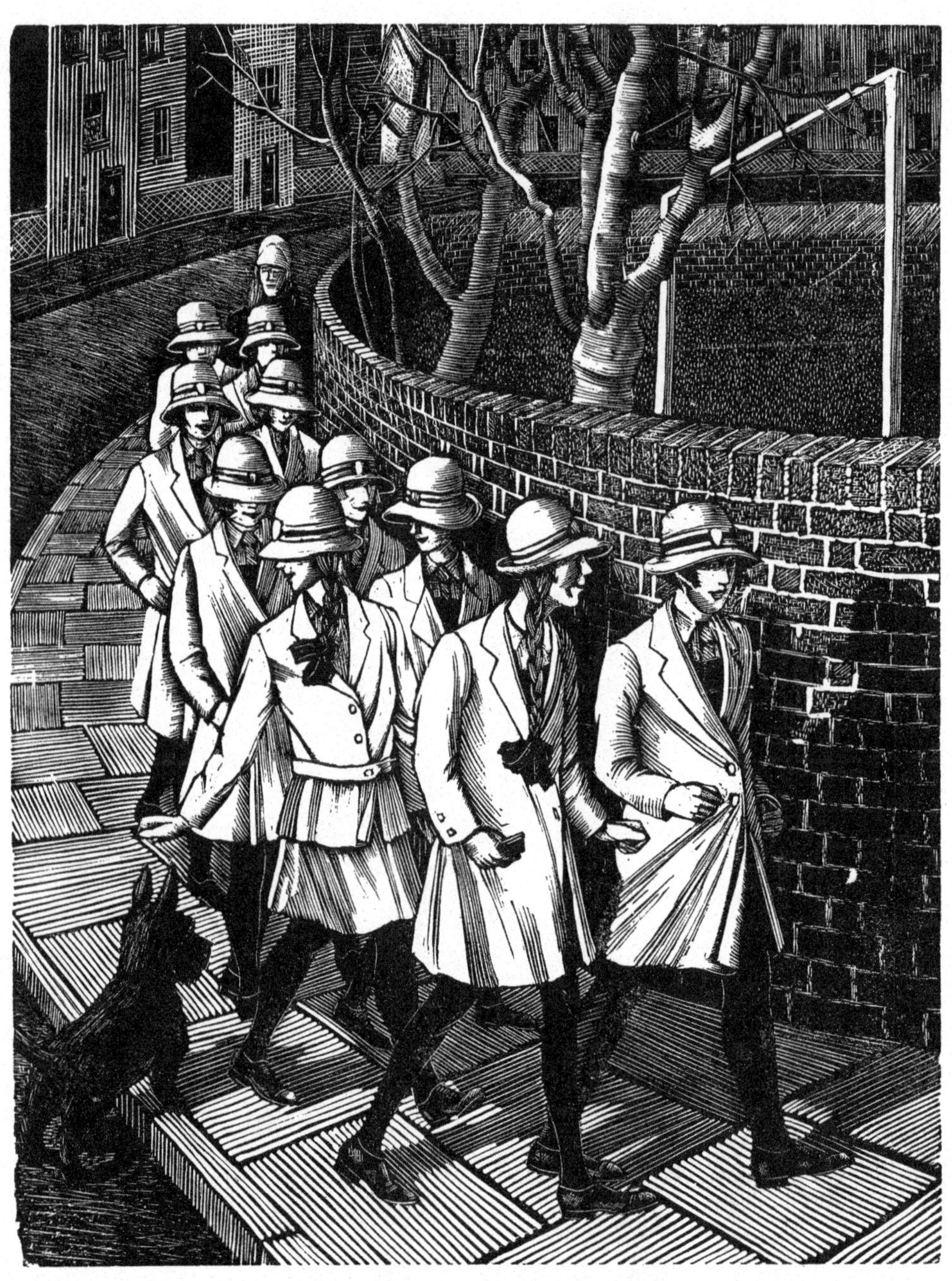

The Crocodile, 1929

TIRZAH GARWOOD

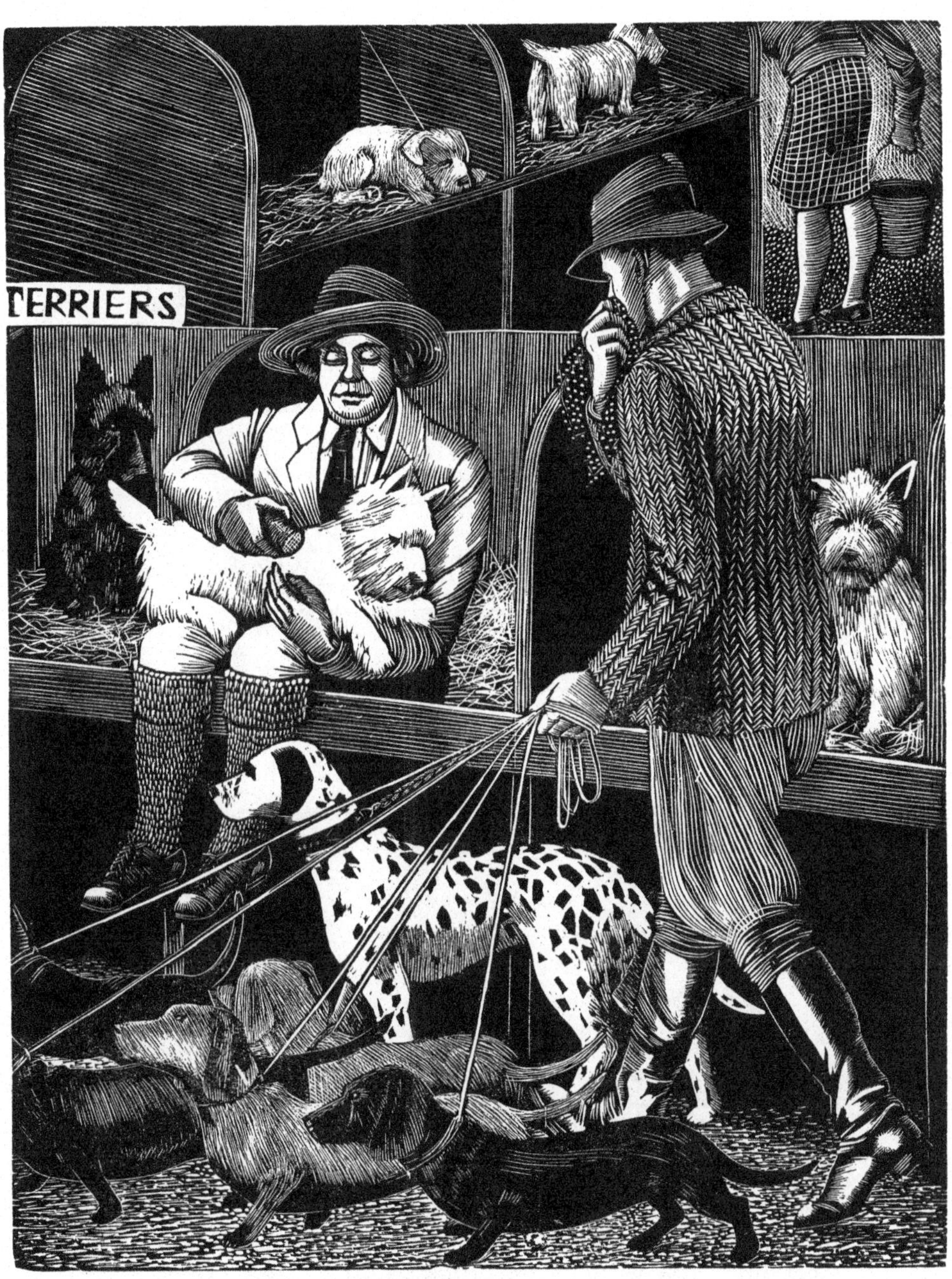

The Dog Show, 1929

TIRZAH GARWOOD

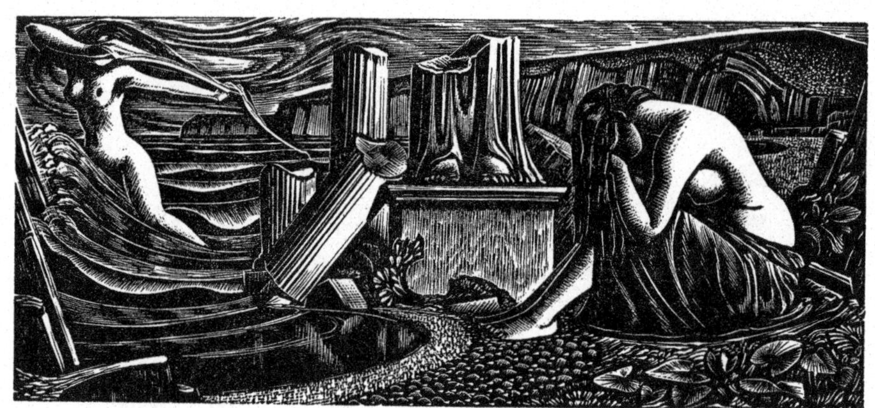

Headpiece from *Hymn to Proserpine* (Golden Cockerel Press, 1944)

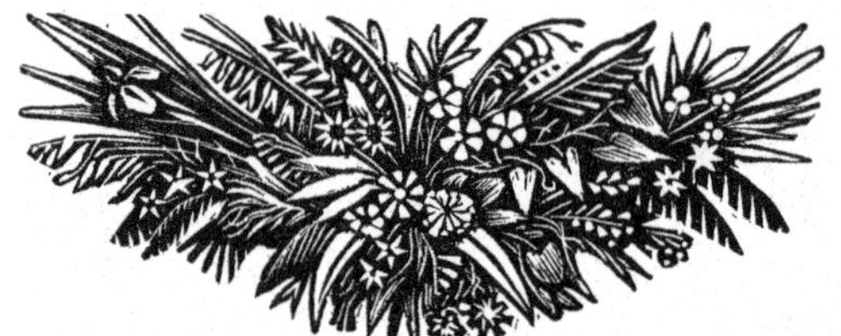

Tailpiece, 1949

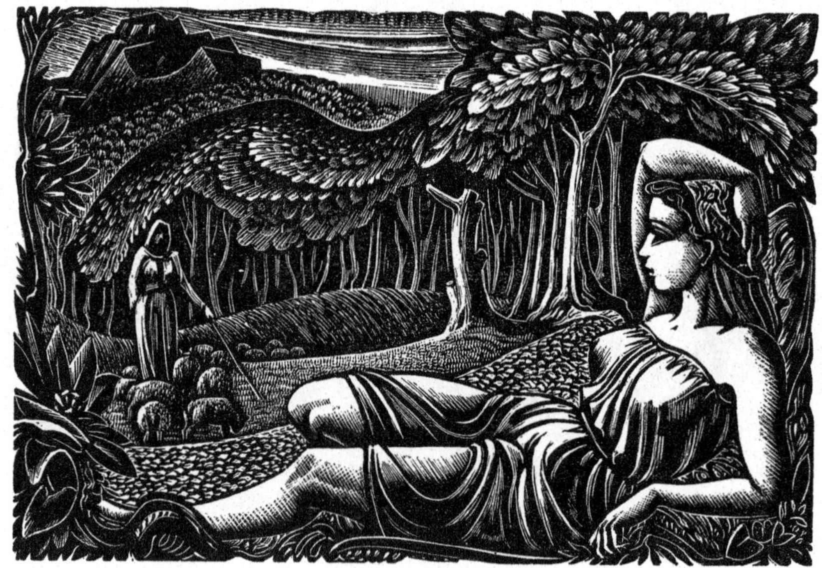

Engraving for *Endymion* (Golden Cockerel Press, 1947)

JOHN BUCKLAND-WRIGHT

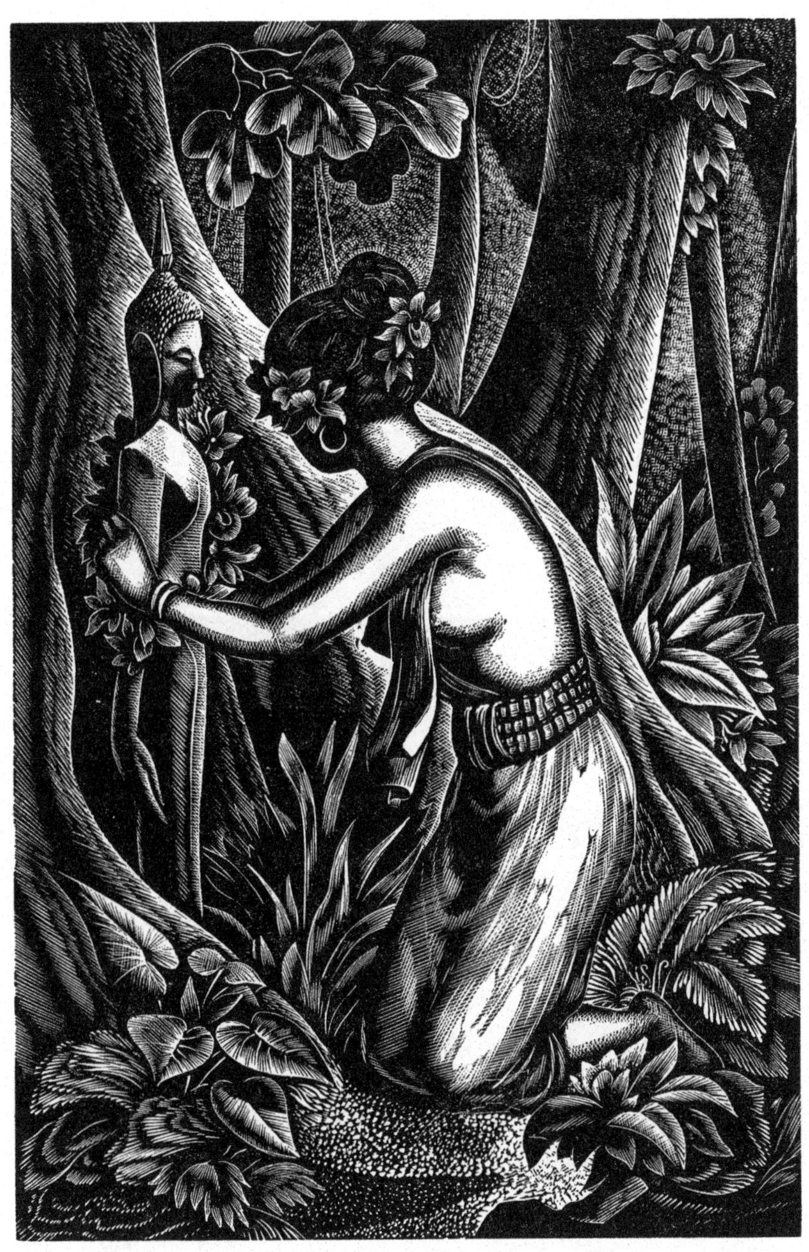

An engraving from *Love Night* by Powys Mathers

(Golden Cockerel Press, 1936)

JOHN BUCKLAND-WRIGHT

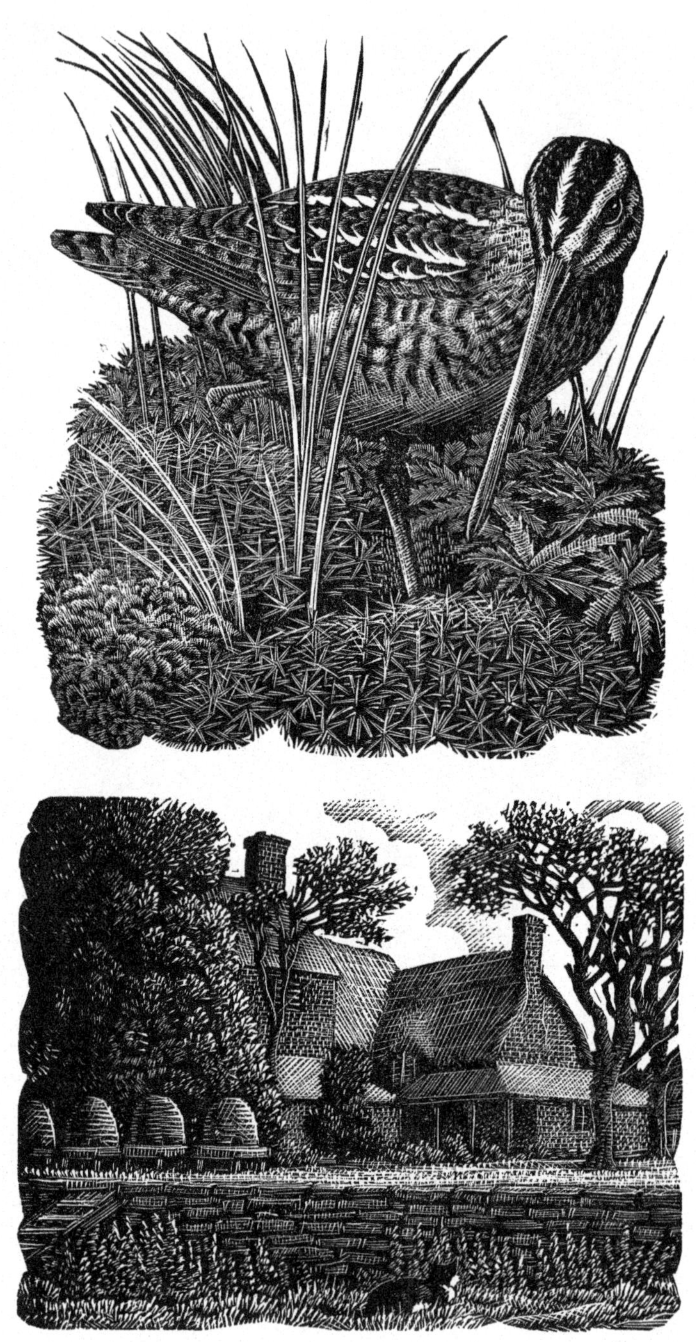

C. F. TUNNICLIFFE. Engravings from *A Book of Birds* (Gollancz, 1937)

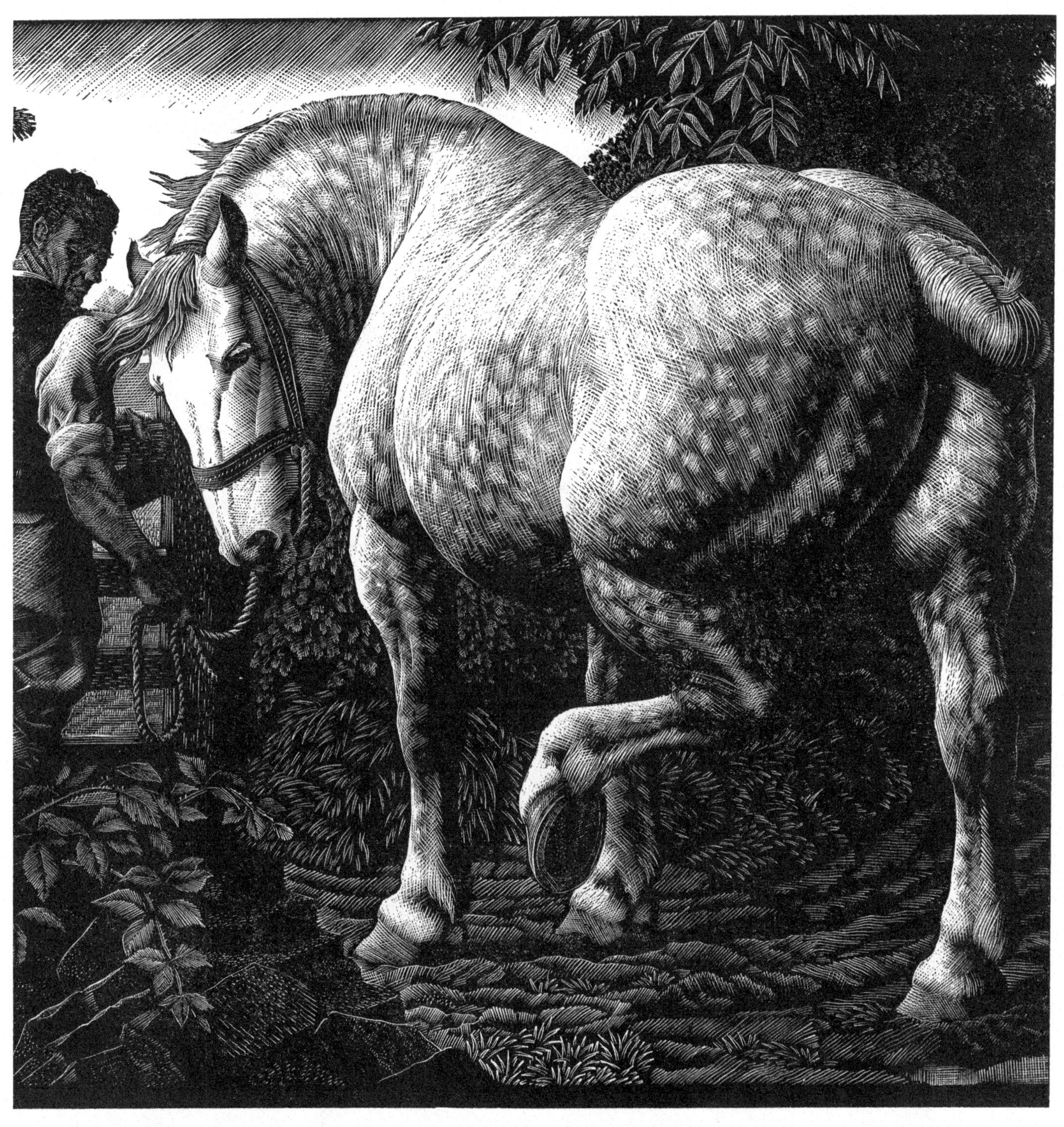

C. F. TUNNICLIFFE. A section of an engraving, *The Percheron Horse*, 1940

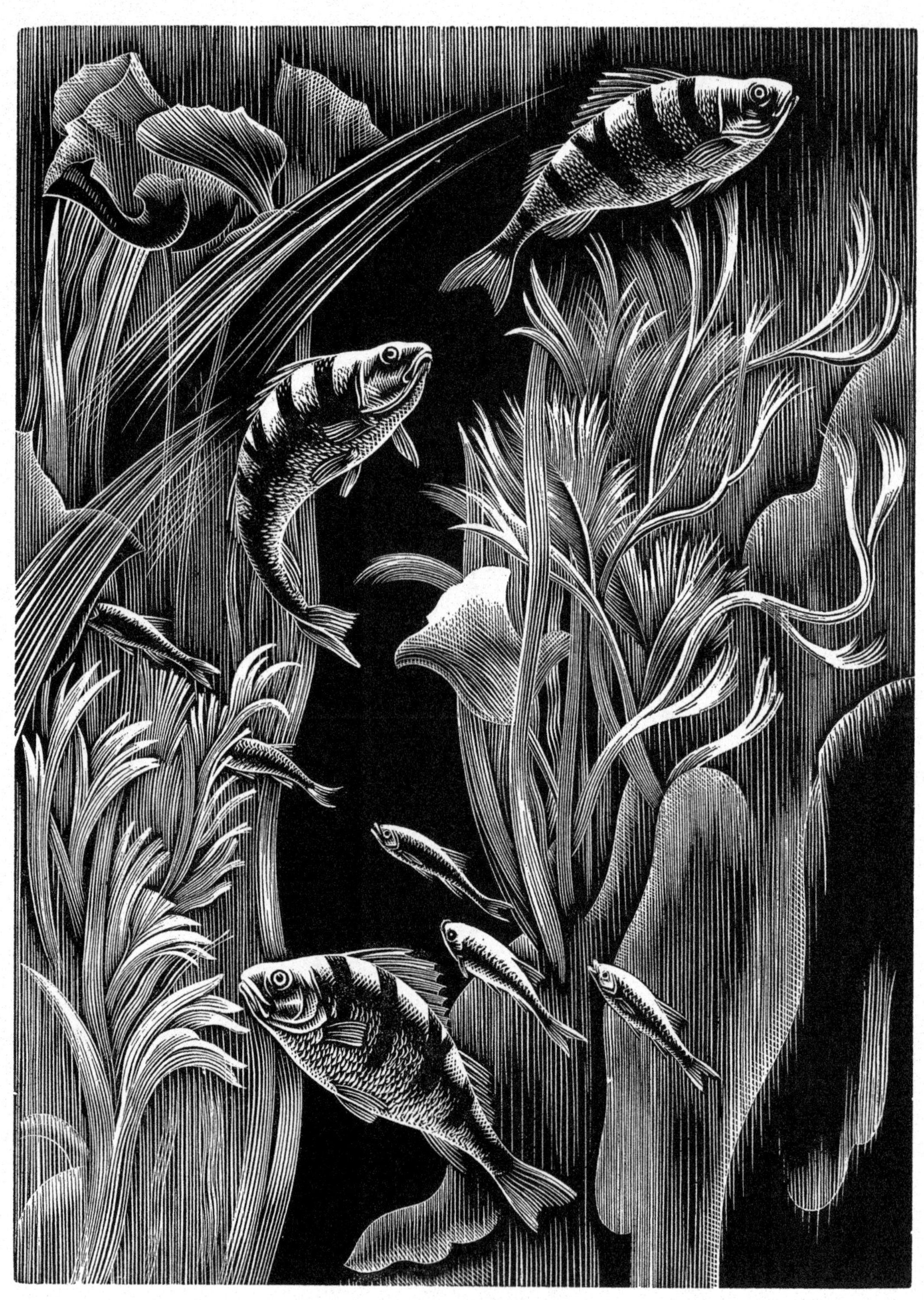

CLIFFORD WEBB. Aquarium, 1934

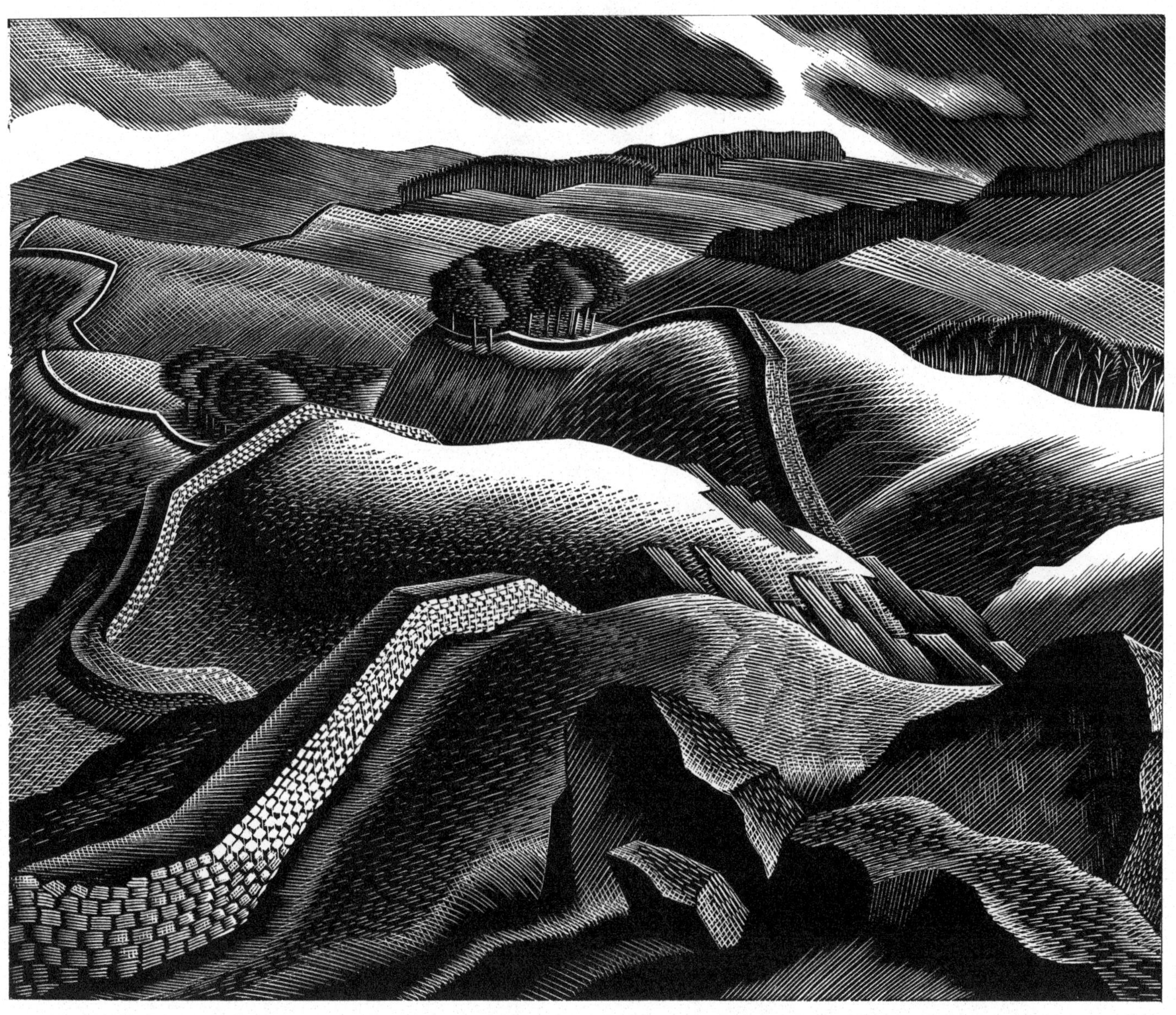

Roman Wall, 1945

CLIFFORD WEBB

OVERLEAF: CLIFFORD WEBB. Pumas, 1949 →

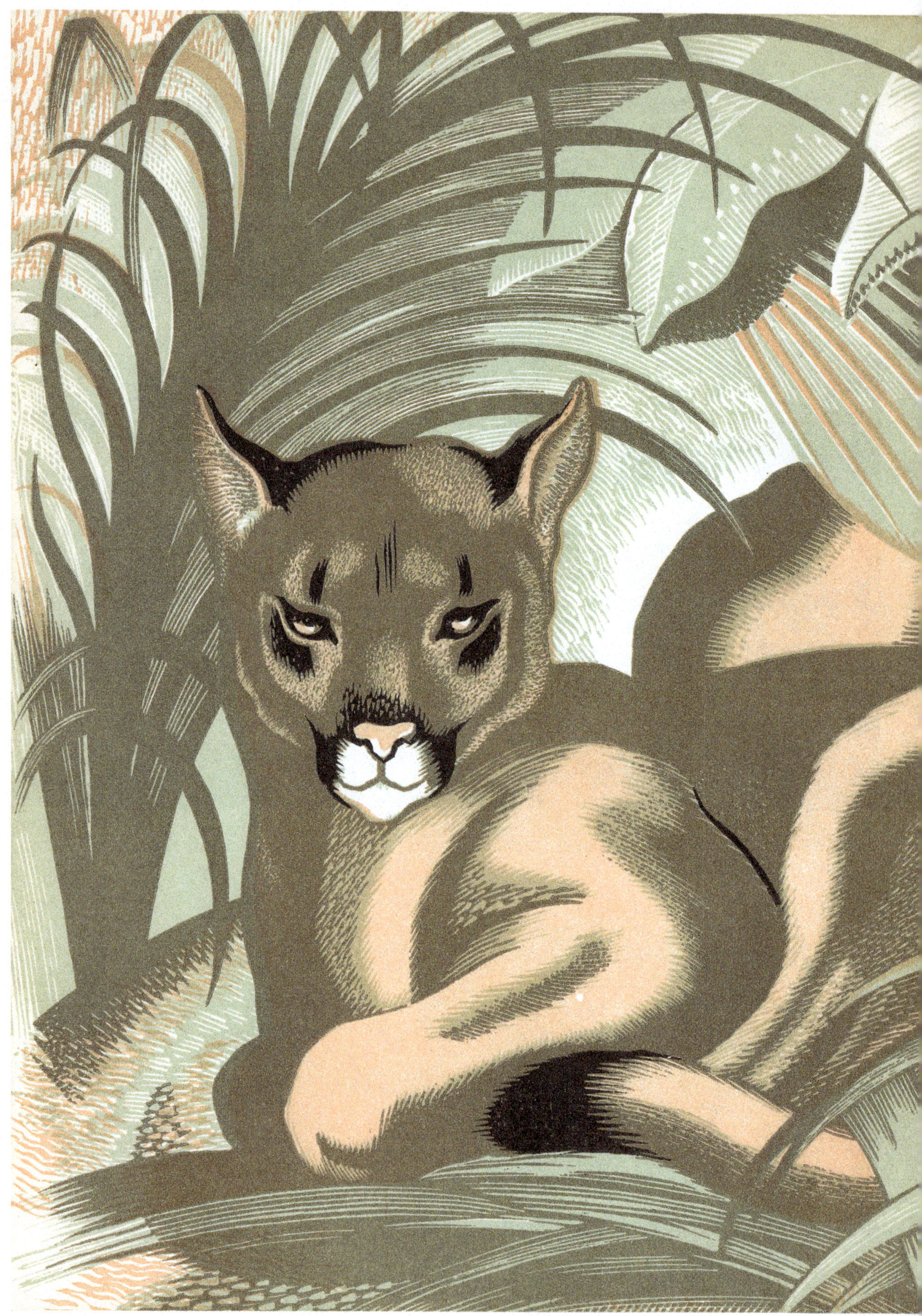

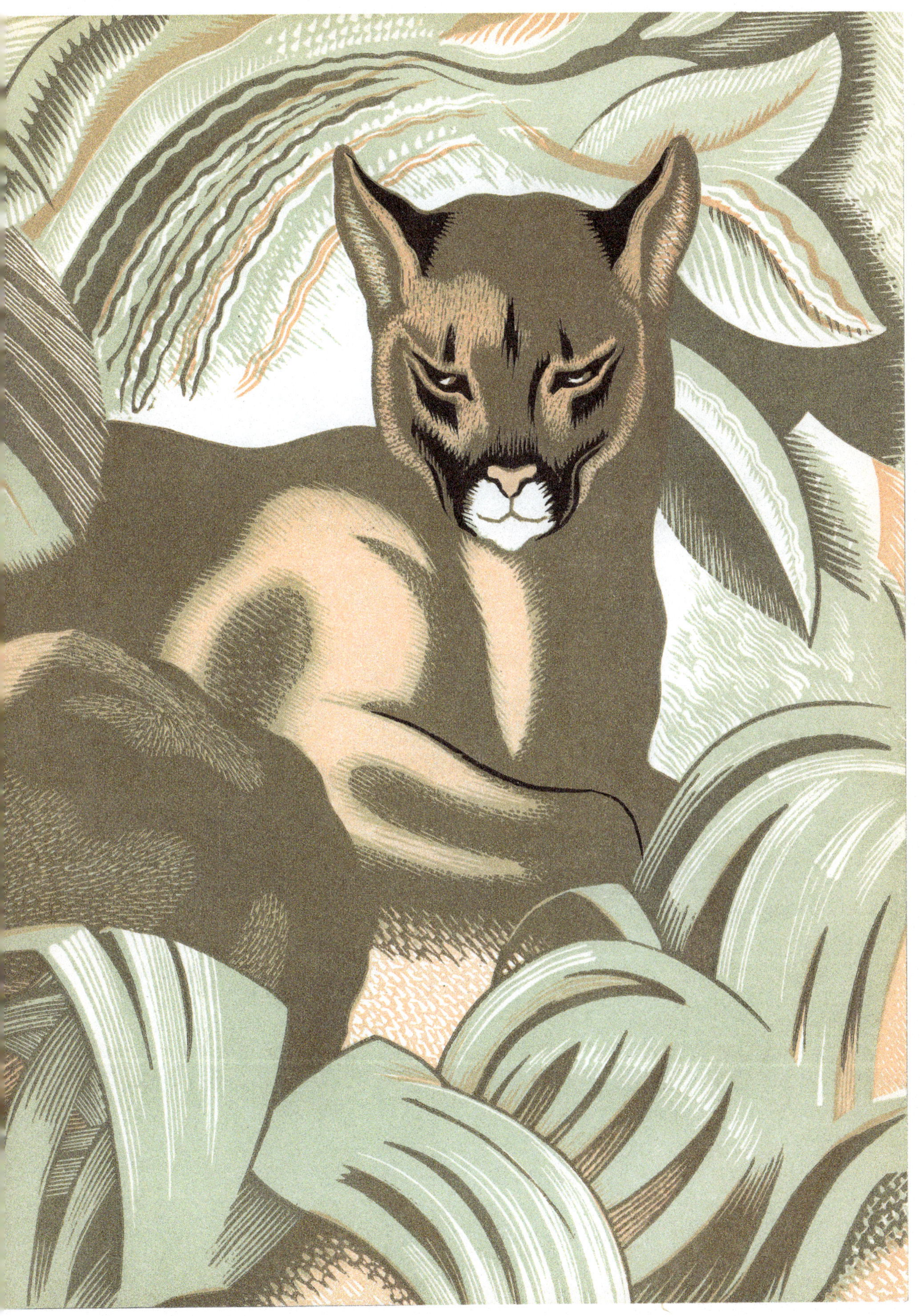

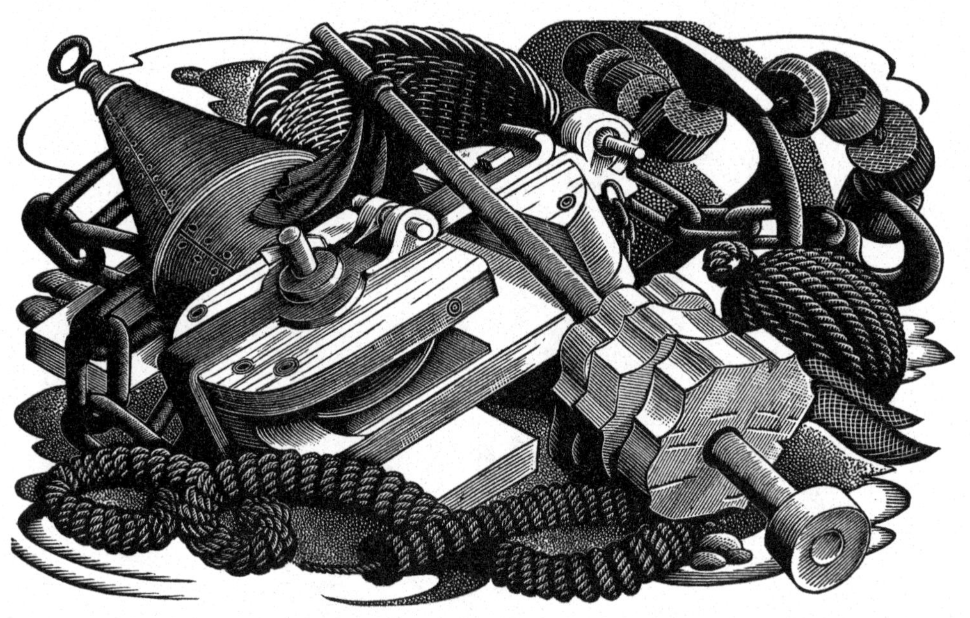

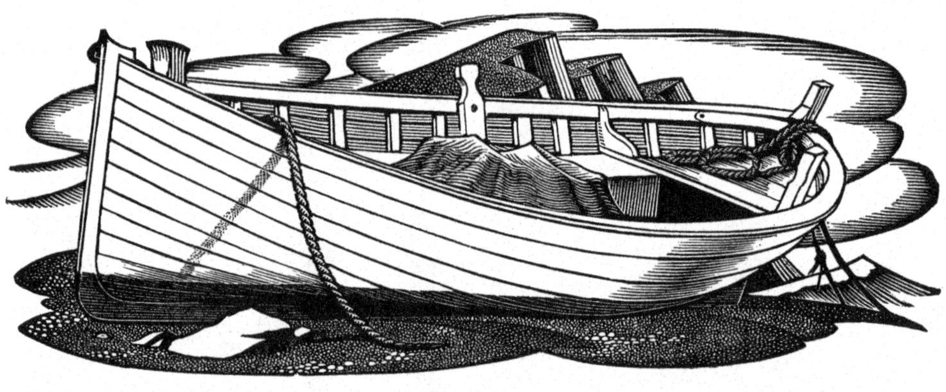

ABOVE AND OPPOSITE PAGE: Three engravings from the artist's book *Wood Engraving* published by the National Magazine Company, 1948

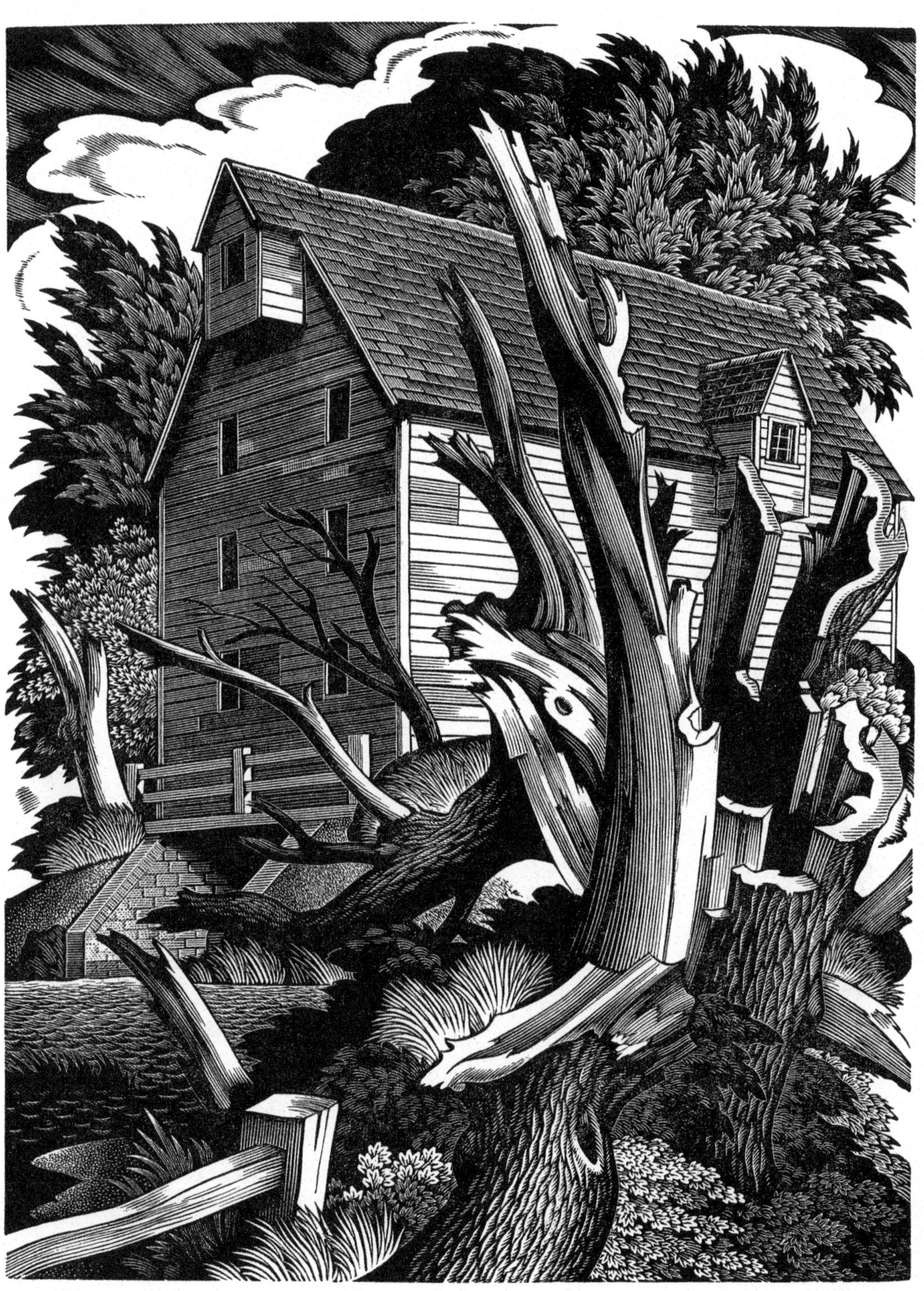

GEORGE E. MACKLEY. The Mill, 1946

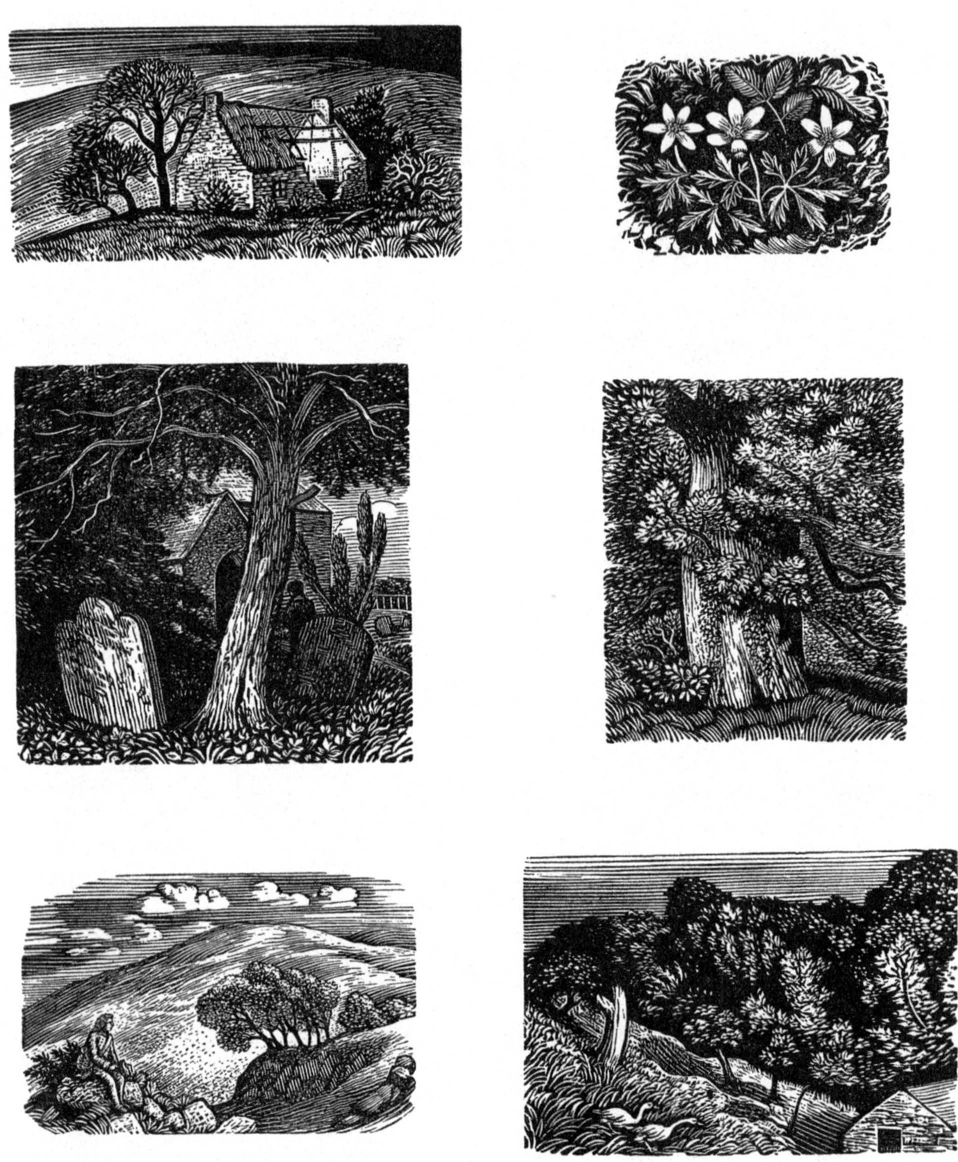

From *The Open Air* by Adrian Bell (Faber, 1946)

REYNOLDS STONE

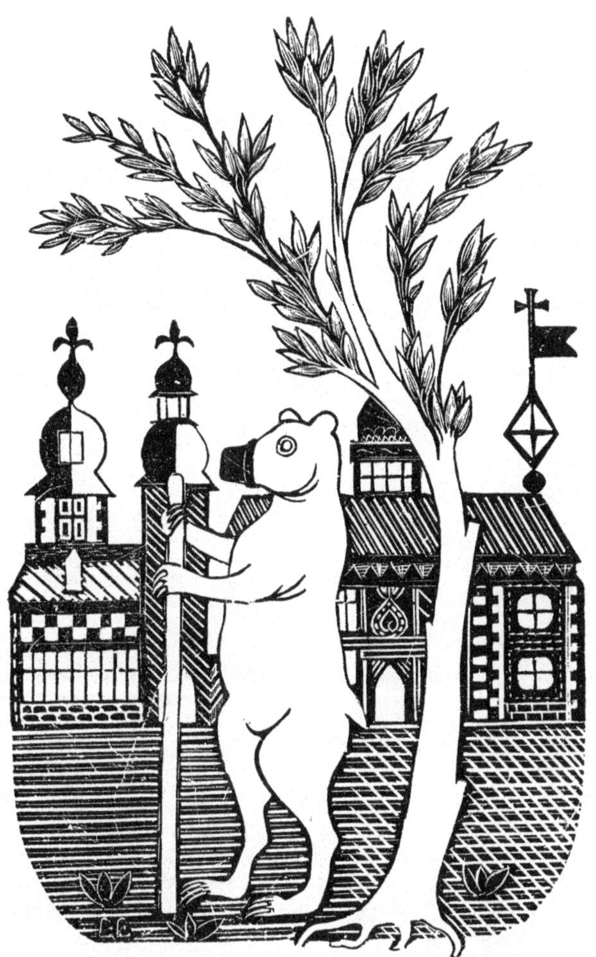

LYNTON LAMB. A device for the Nonesuch Press, 1935

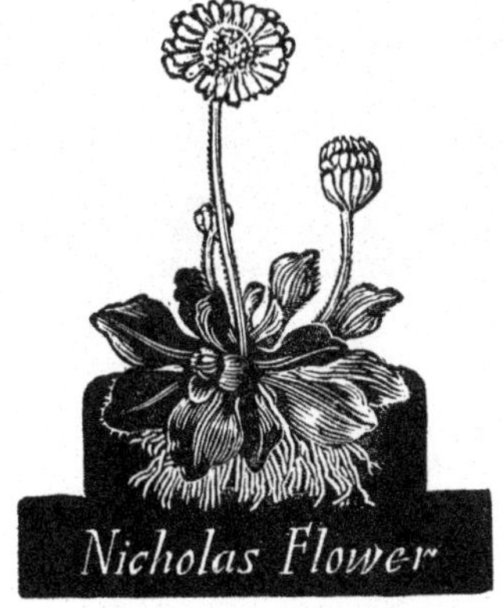

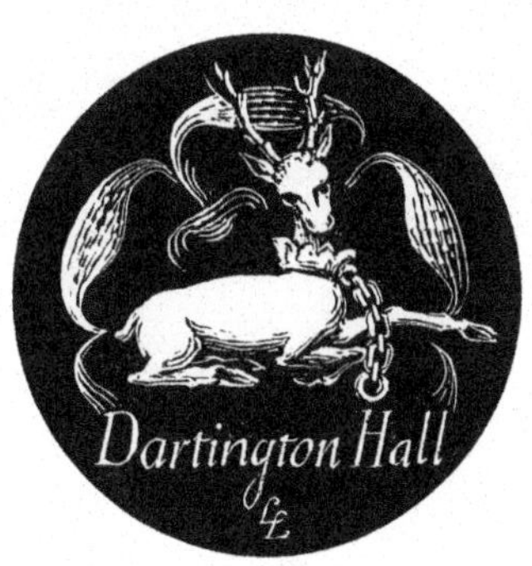

Two bookplates, 1949-50
LYNTON LAMB

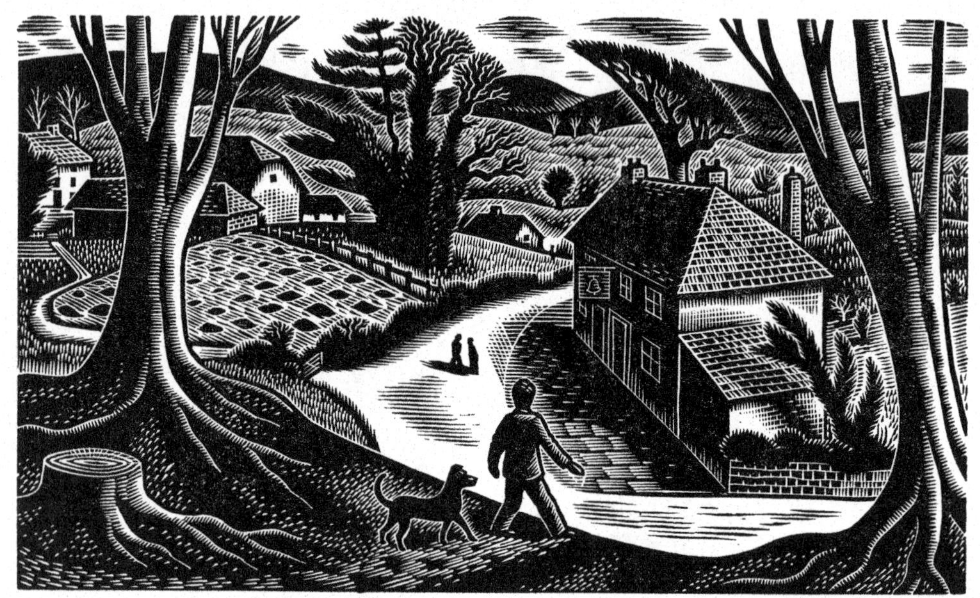

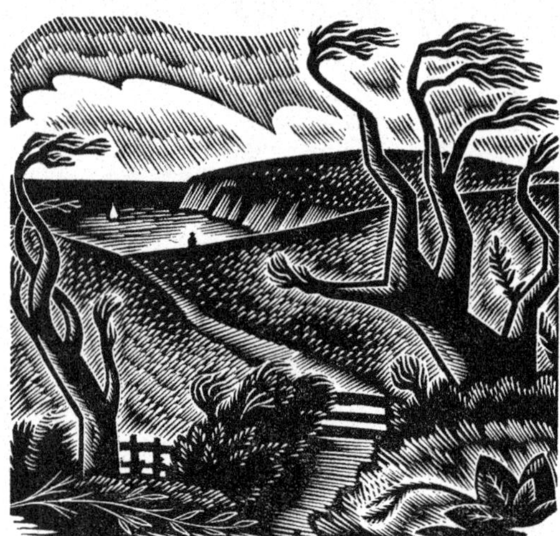

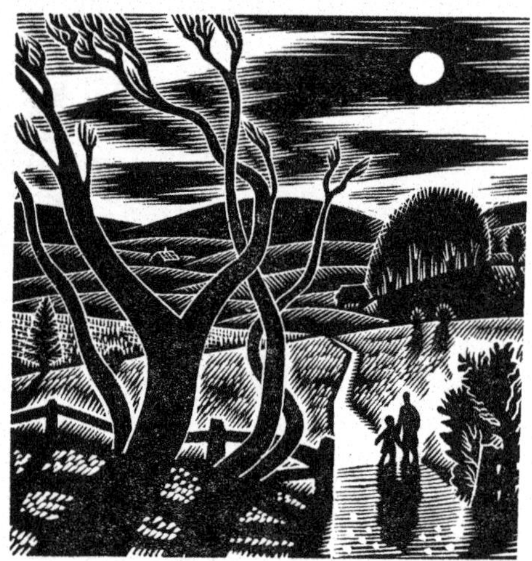

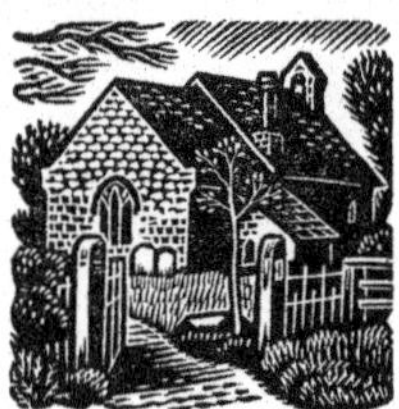

GWENDA MORGAN. Country Scenes, 1940-50

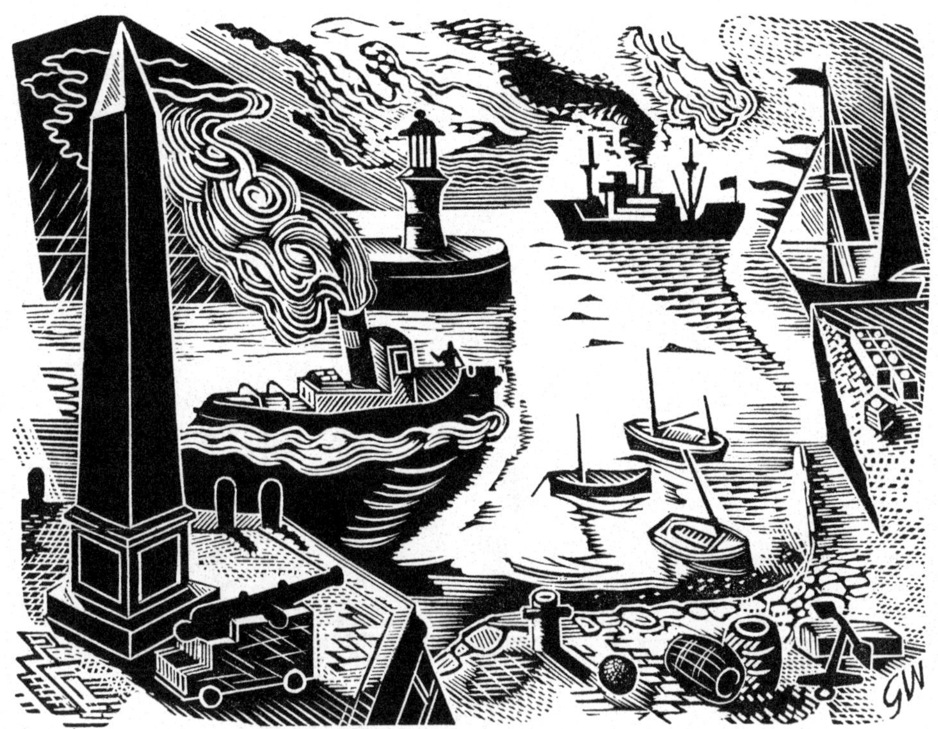

GEOFFREY WALES. Design for Export edition of *Harper's Bazaar*, 1949

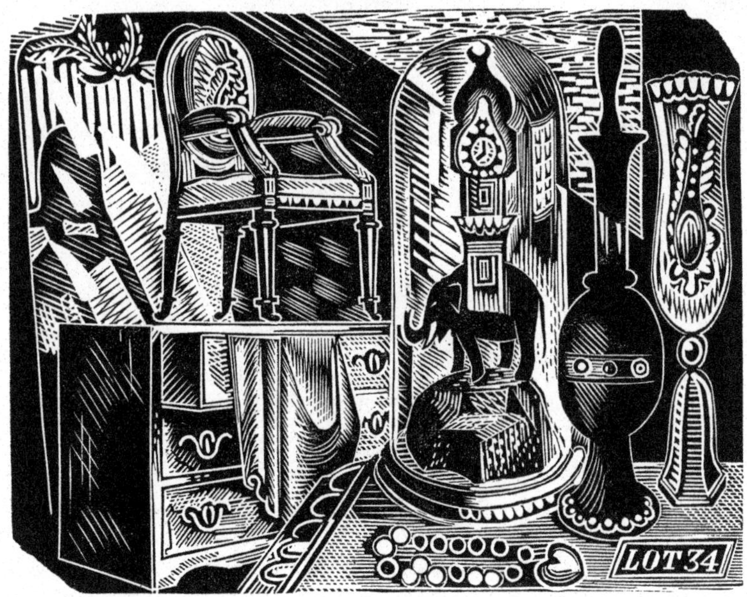

GEOFFREY WALES. Lot 34 (Kynoch Press, 1948)

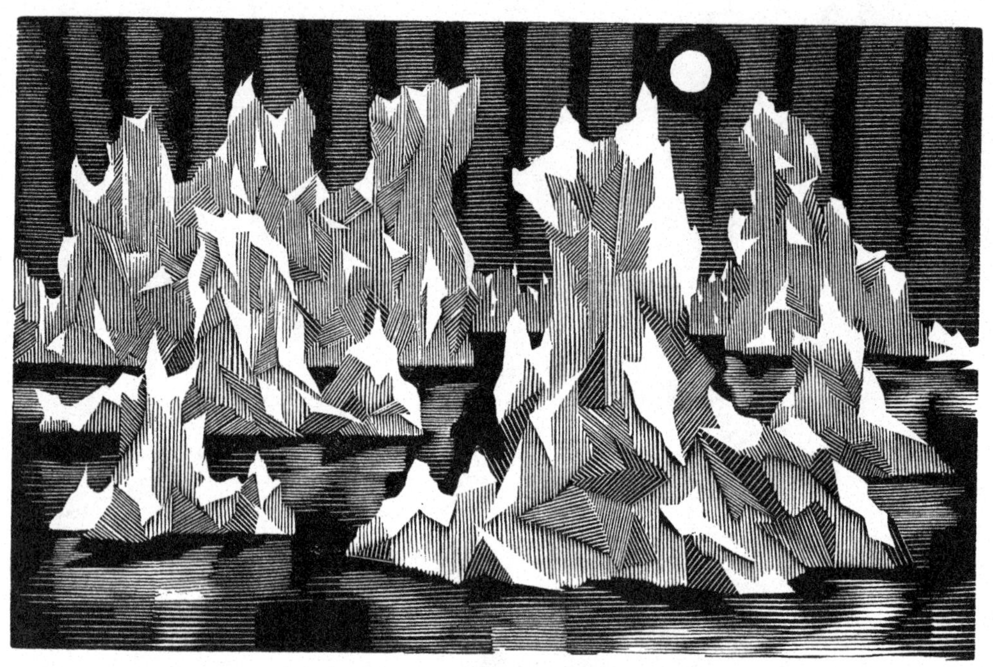

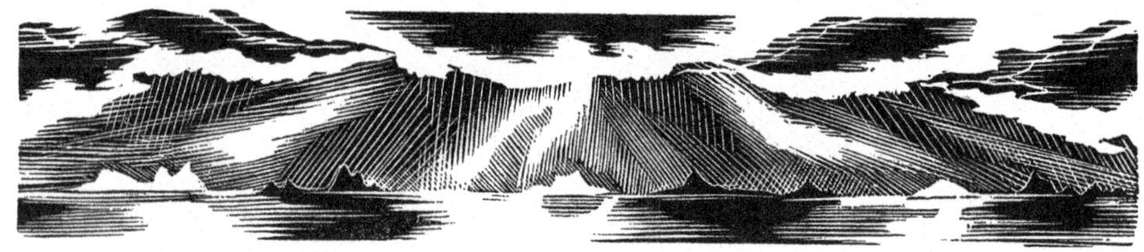

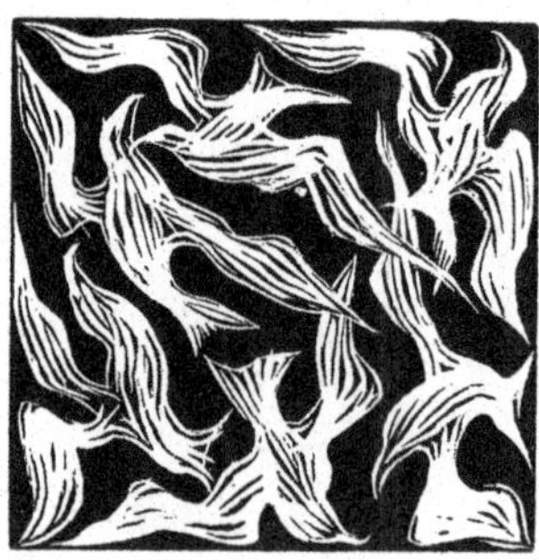

PETER BARKER-MILL. From *A Voyage Round the World* (Golden Cockerel Press, 1944)

OPPOSITE PAGE: WINIFRED MCKENZIE. House over the Canal, Bath, 1950 →

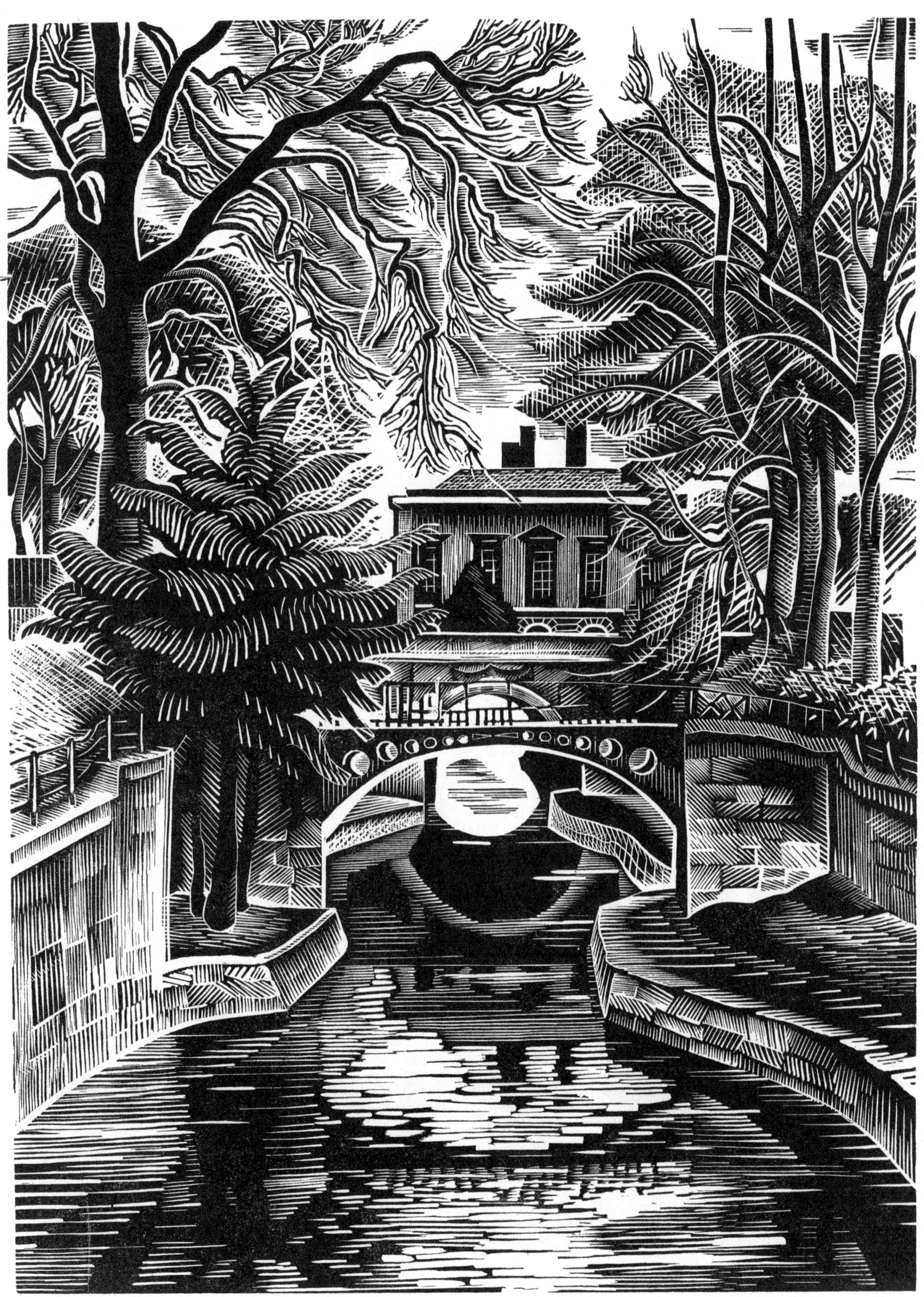

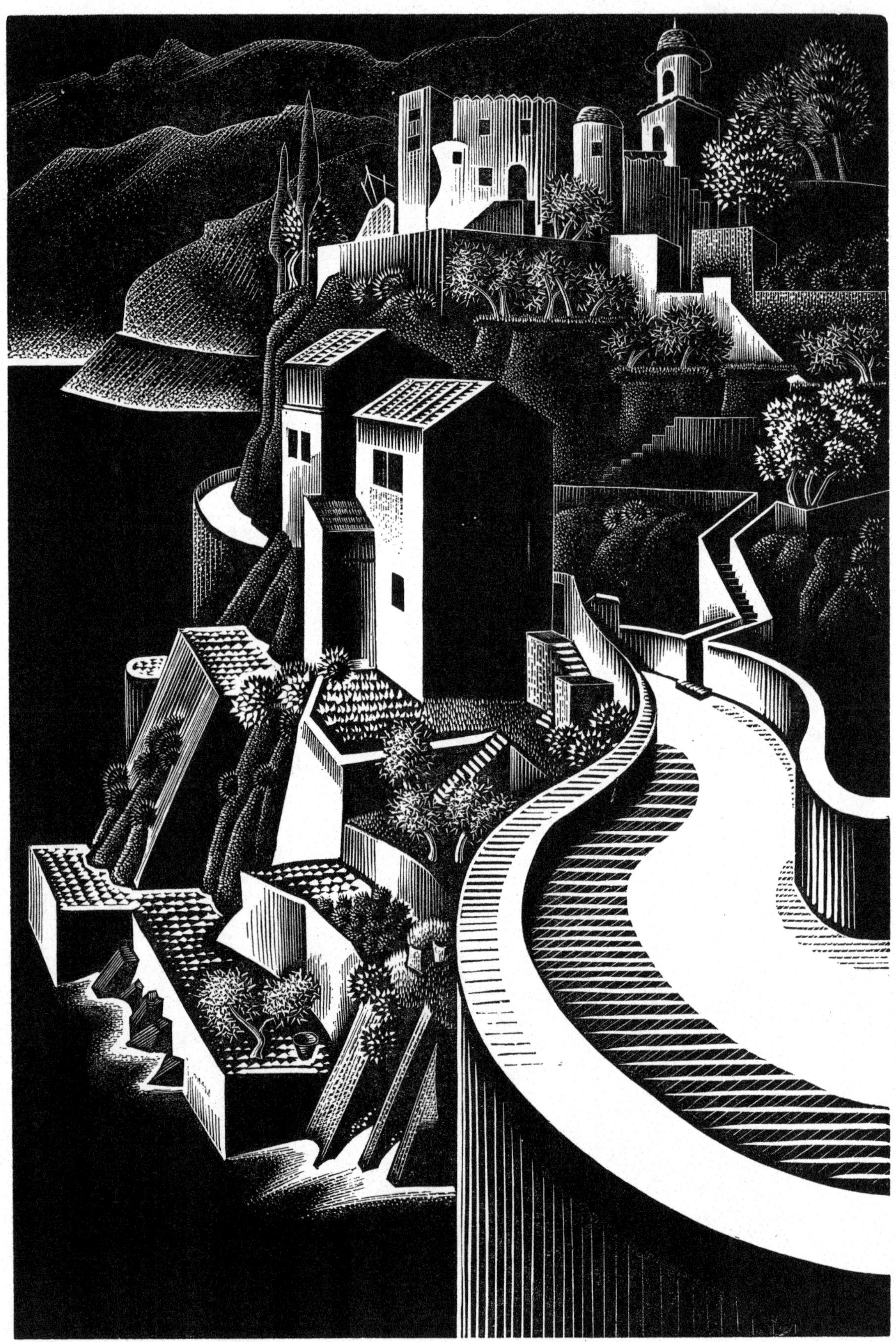

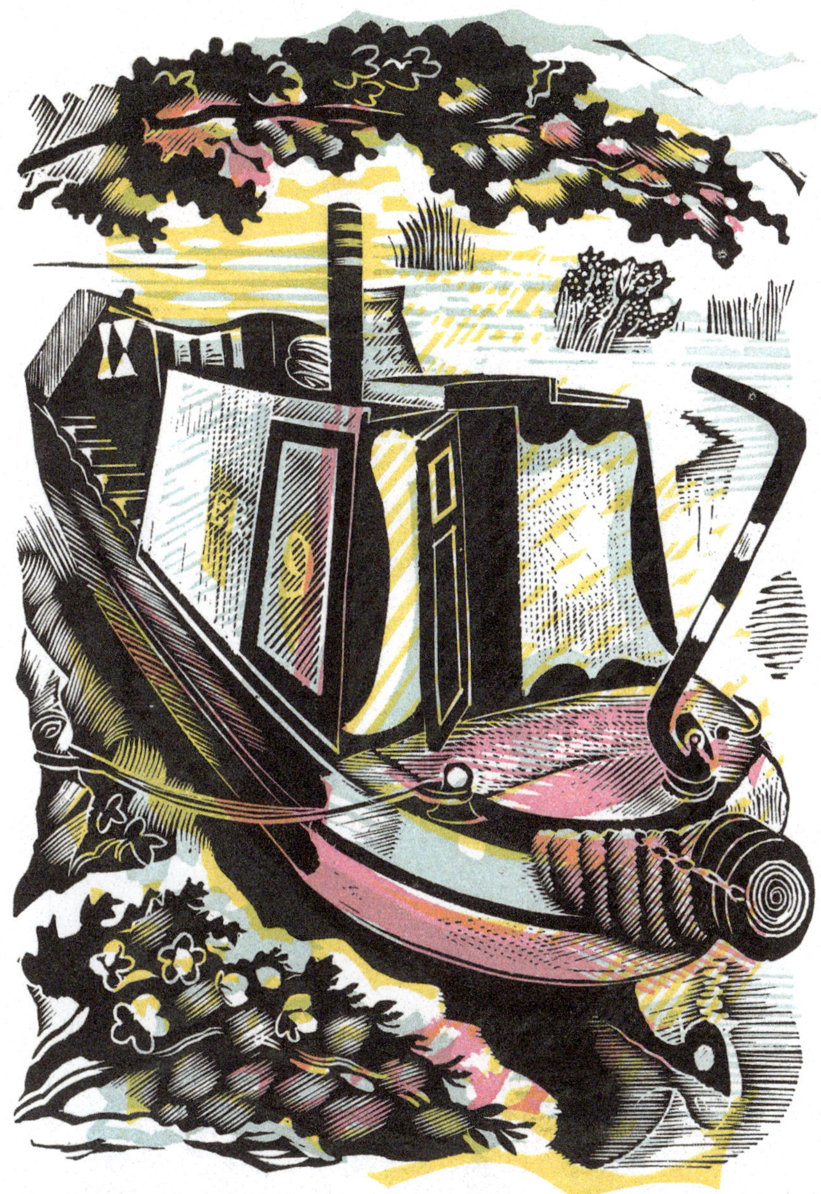

From *Canals, Barges and People* (Art and Technics, 1950)

JOHN O'CONNOR

← ALISON MACKENZIE. The Road to Sorrento

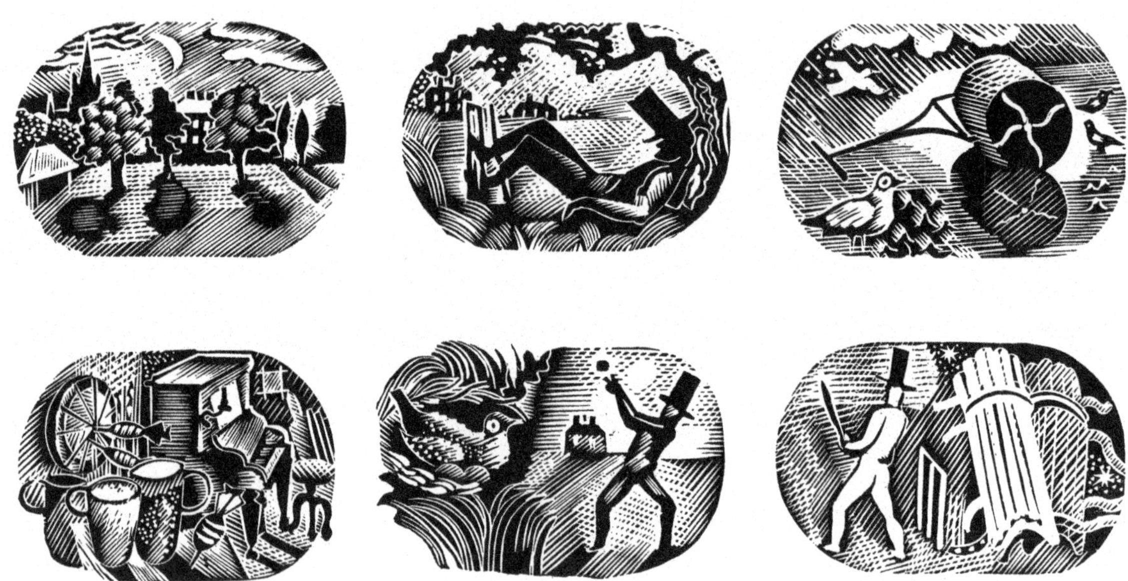

JOHN O'CONNOR. Headpieces from *The Young Cricketer's Tutor* (Dropmore Press, 1948)

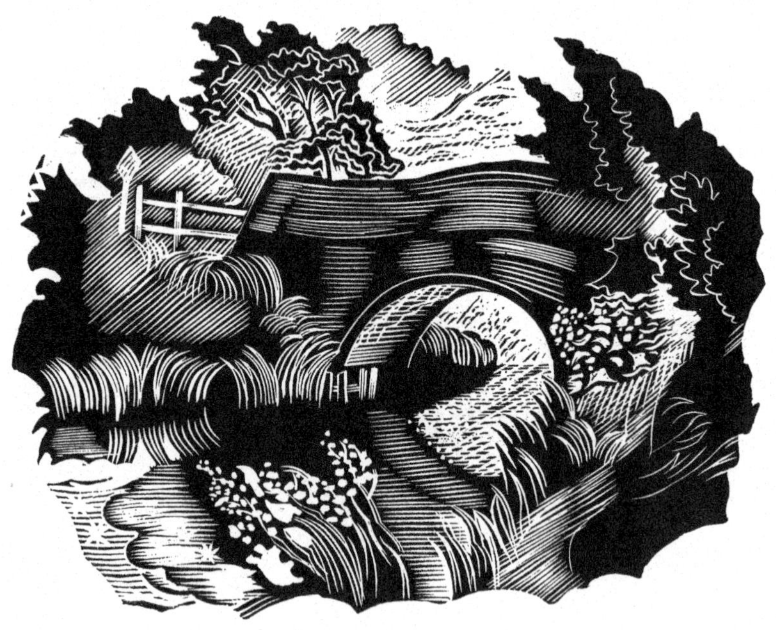

JOHN O'CONNOR. From *Canals, Barges and People* (Art and Technics, 1950)

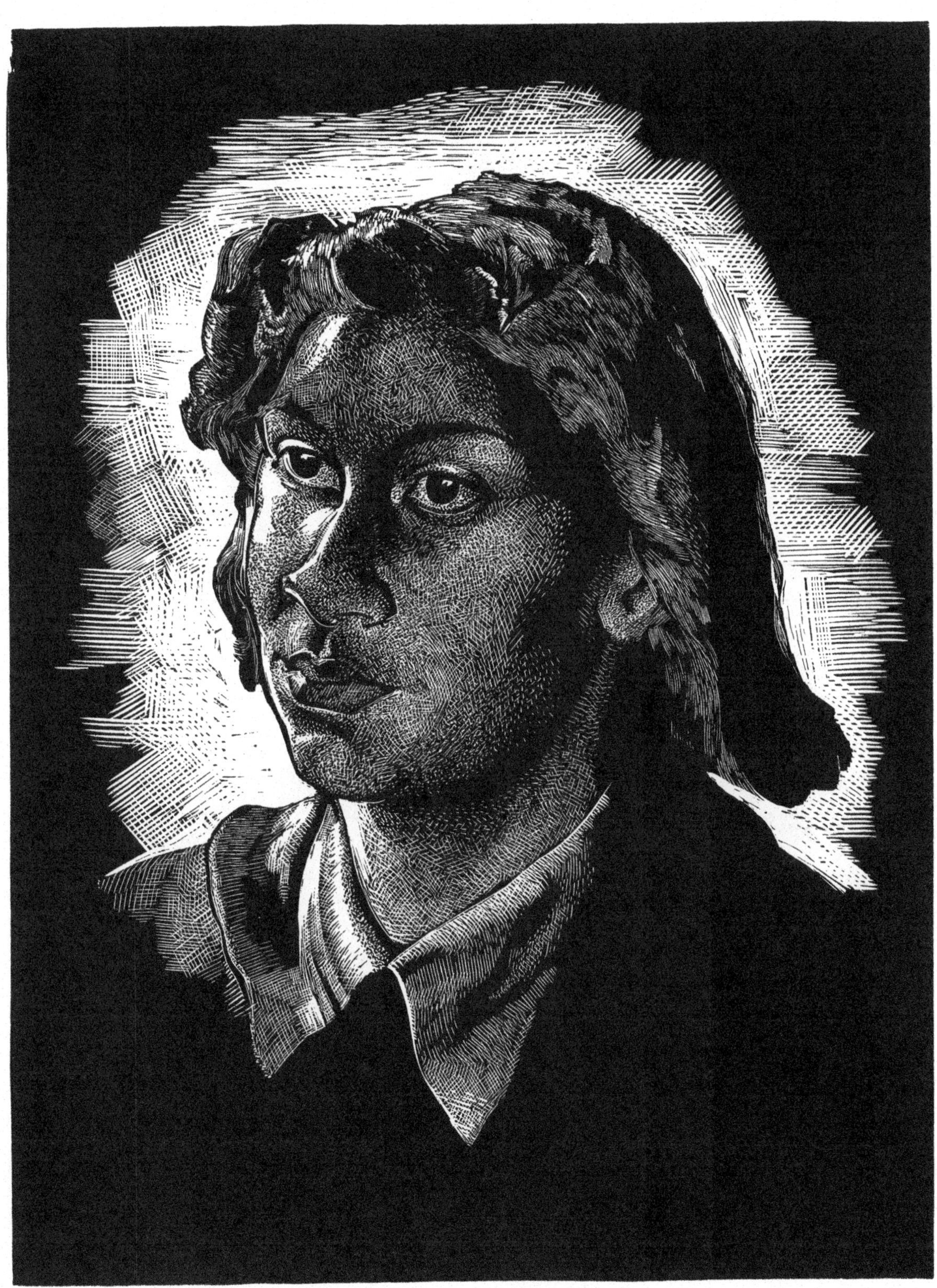

WILLIAM ARMOUR. Girl's Head, 1949

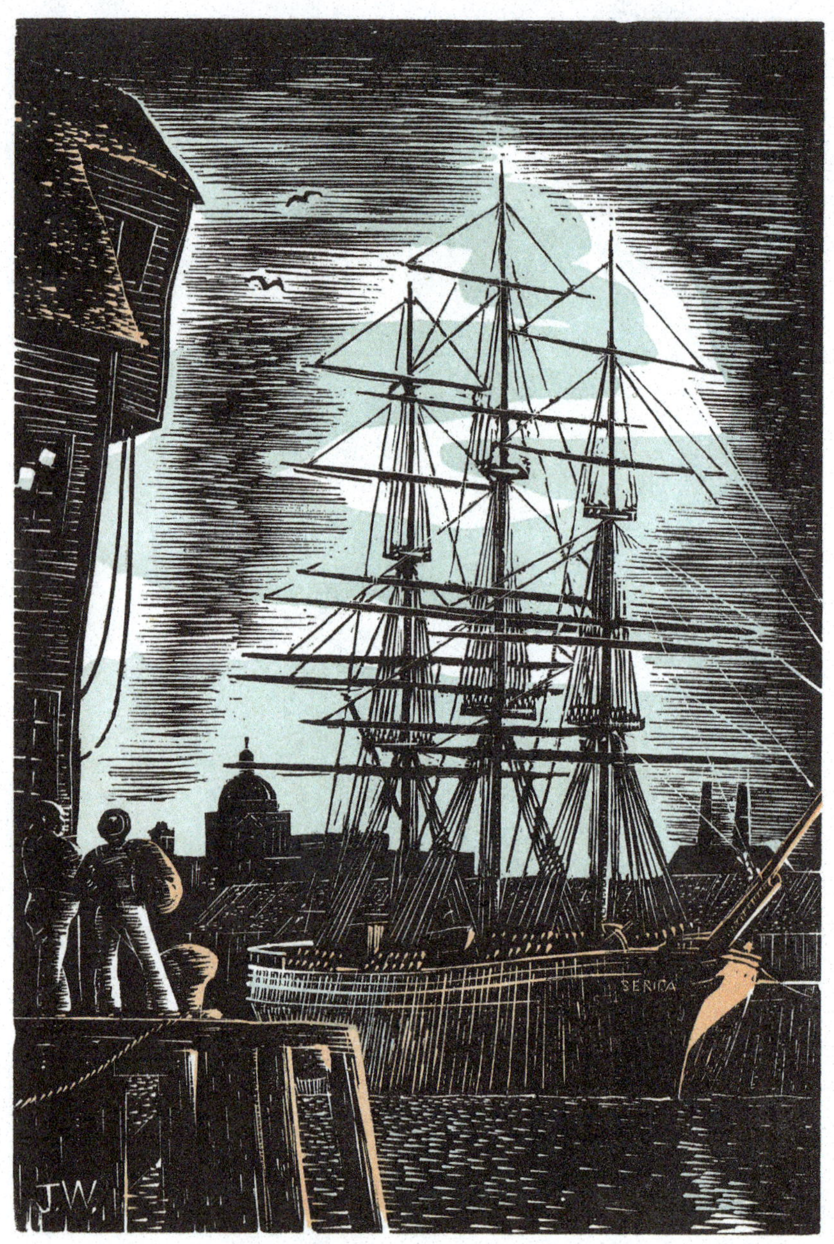

Engraving for *The Wreck of the Serica*
published by The Dropmore Press, 1950

JOHN WORSLEY

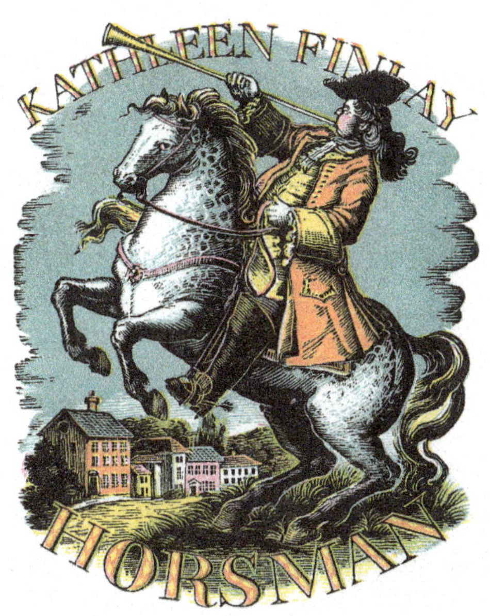

Bookplate for Kathleen Finlay Horsman, 1946

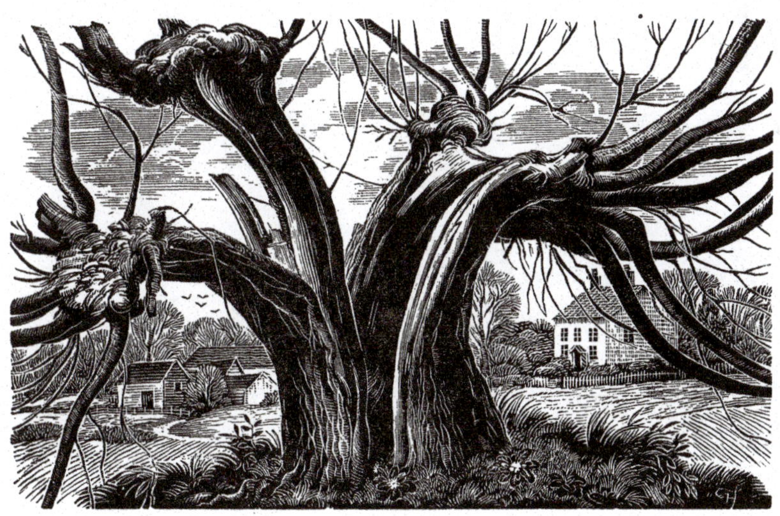

From *Our Village* by Mary Russell Mitford (Harrap, 1946)

JOAN HASSALL

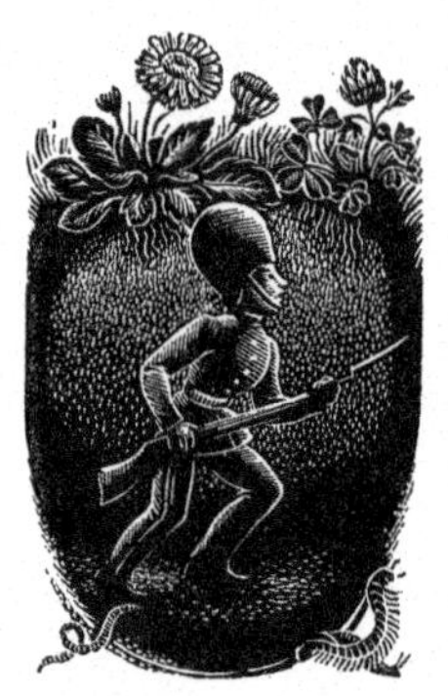

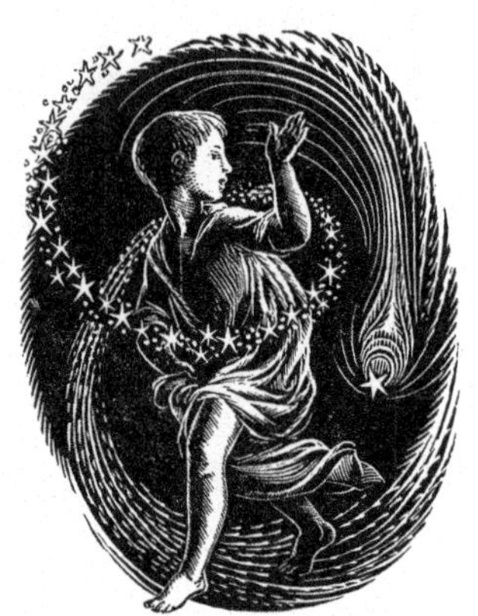

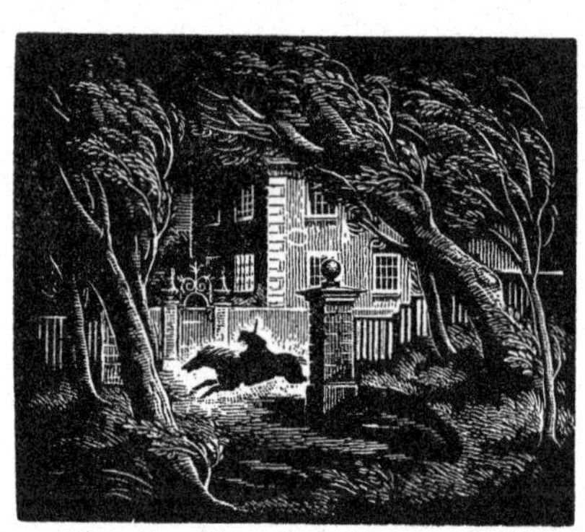

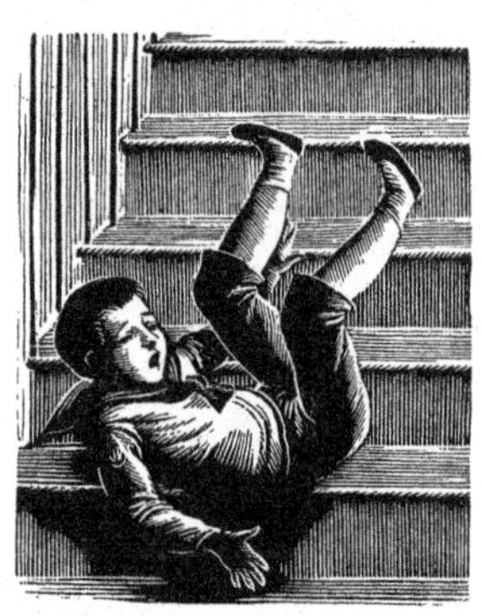

From *Child's Garden of Verses* (Hopetown Press)

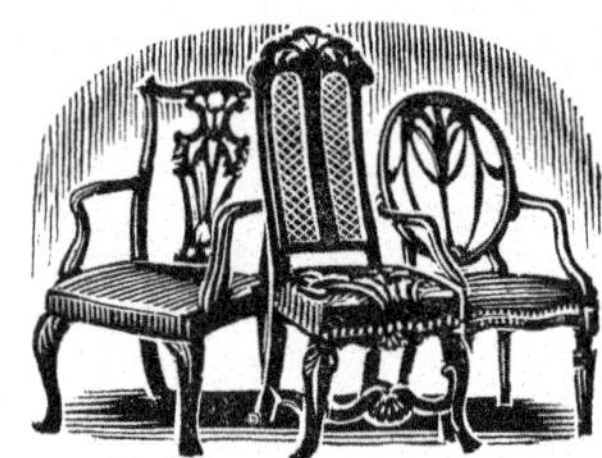

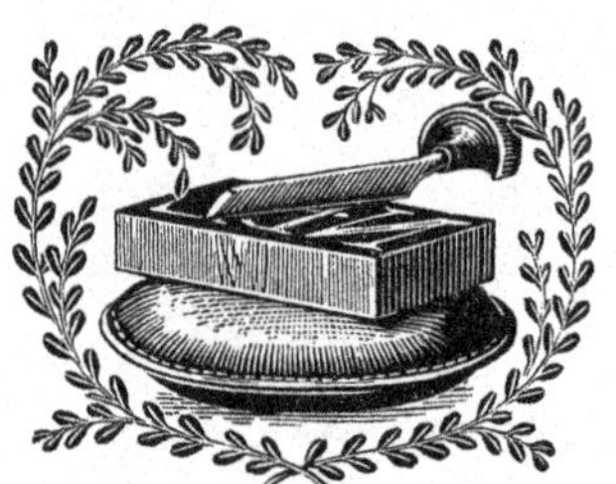

From National Book League Bibliographies, 1945-50

JOAN HASSALL

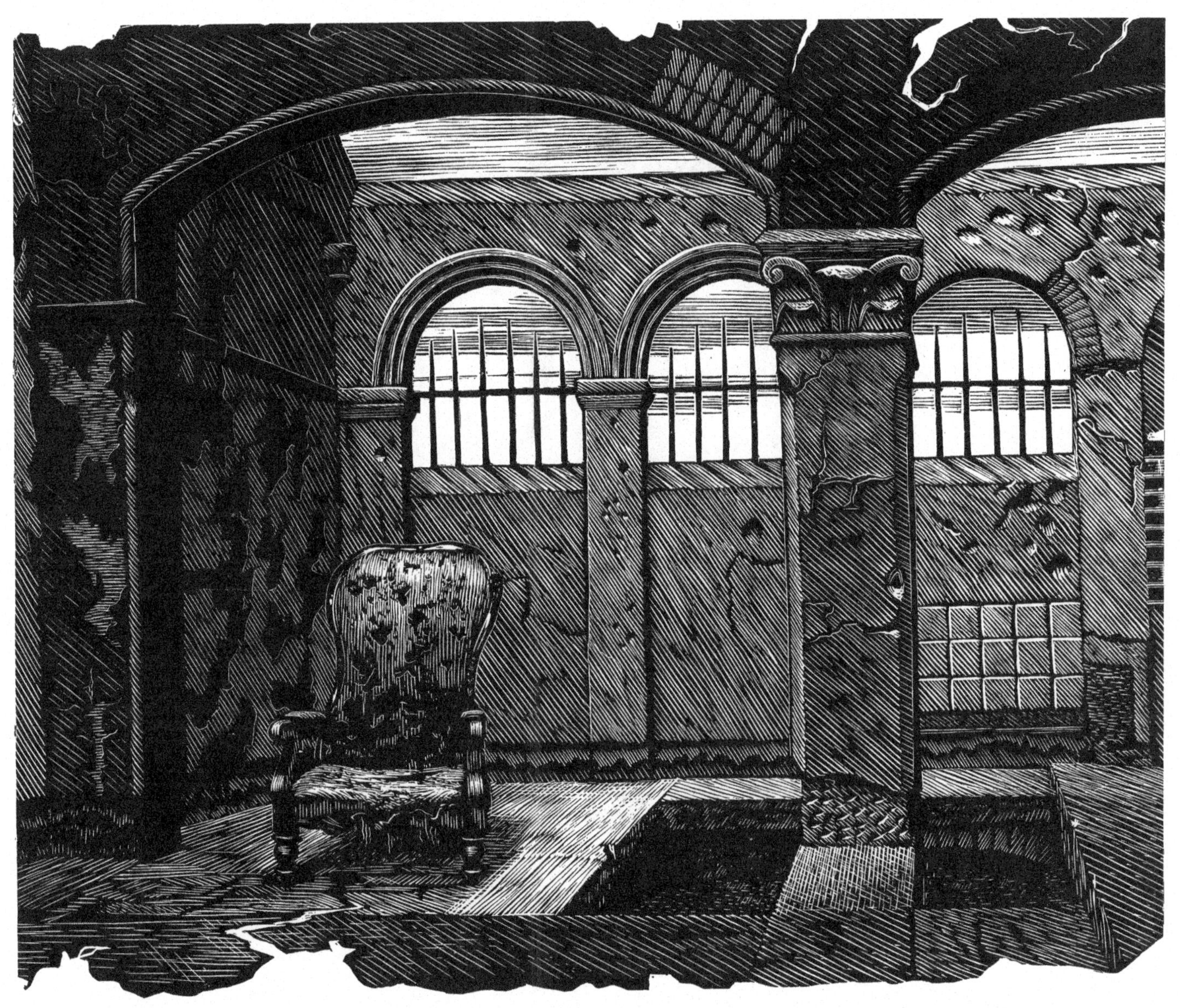

The House with the Tattered Wallpaper, 1949

KINGSLEY COOK

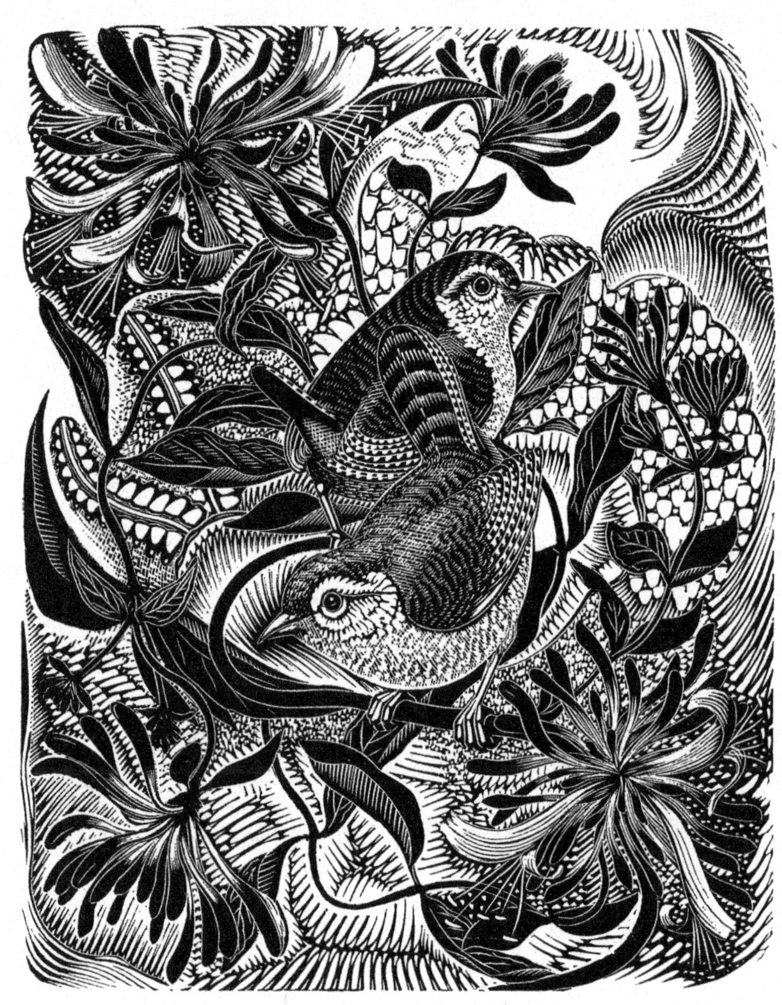

Wrens in Honeysuckle

G. W. LENNOX PATERSON